MIND THE

3rd Edition

GETTING BUSINESS RESULTS IN
MULTIGENERATIONAL ORGANIZATIONS

CURTIS L. ODOM, ED.D.

Book·nol·o·gy
n. delivering useable information and knowledge
that adds value to people's lives

A BUSINESS & EDUCATIONAL IMPRINT FROM ADDUCENT
WWW.ADDUCENTCREATIVE.COM

TITLES DISTRIBUTED IN
NORTH AMERICA
UNITED KINGDOM
WESTERN EUROPE
SOUTH AMERICA
AUSTRALIA
CHINA
INDIA

MIND THE GAP

GETTING BUSINESS RESULTS IN MULTIGENERATIONAL ORGANIZATIONS

Curtis L. Odom, Ed.D.

THIRD EDITION

PAPERBACK ISBN: 9781937592455

PUBLISHED BY BOOKNOLOGY (A BUSINESS AND EDUCATIONAL IMPRINT FROM ADDUCENT)

JACKSONVILLE, FLORIDA

WWW.ADDUCENTCREATIVE.COM

DEDICATION

To my beautiful wife and best friend for life, Nelia. You are my creative muse. I am again reminded that there is no 'me' without you. As we start yet another chapter in our incredible story, your willingness to always listen continues to inspire me. This book, my 4th, is yet another dream that took shape as an idea, which turned into months of early mornings and late nights as I went about the work of writing it. You are my reason for everything. Your fingerprints are on my every success. I cannot imagine this world without you to share every experience. Your love for me is the song in my heart. I love you!

To my lovely daughter and best giggle buddy, Alyssa. I've watched you grow from an adorable little girl into a charming and lovely young lady. And every day I am prouder of you. It is a blessing and a privilege to have you as my daughter. We are so much alike, in so many ways. I aspire daily to be your hero, to be your role model for the type of leader I hope you will one day become. I hope this book will remind you one day, long after I am gone, that your Dad took the greatest joys of his life from moments spent looking at the world through your smiling eyes while sitting next to you at sunset on a Cape Cod beach. I love you!

ACKNOWLEDGMENTS

I would like to express my deepest appreciation for the unwavering support of my editor, publisher, mentor, and friend, Dennis Lowery, who continues to create an environment in which I was able to explore without boundaries the ongoing practice of the craft of being a published author. His advice and counsel, our shared offbeat sense of humor, and a similar perspective on life and liberty as a Navy veteran is a continued match for my style. Thank you, Dennis, for your partnership, mentoring and coaching to always be true to self while living and writing with the Navy core values of Honor, Courage, and Commitment.

To my mother, Hilda, thank you for all of your love and support. I am grateful for your wisdom and guidance through my formative years. Your love is truly a blessing in my life as I always felt your hand on my shoulder through the darkest nights as both a boy and a young man. Thanks, Mom for everything.

Thanks to my brother-in-law, Hillard, for instilling in me the value of education and the importance of not being satisfied with anything less than my best. As the male role model in my personal life, I continue to aspire to follow the example you have set. Your work ethic, creativity, and a keen eye for all that is possible dared me to achieve. Your prophetic words to me long ago sound in my ear as my mantra when the toughest of life and career obstacles present themselves: *"Short-term inconvenience for long-term gain."* Brown Dawg, you are my hero!

To my sister, Betty; my mother-in-law, Lucia; my father-in-law, Afonso; my sister-in-law, Allison, and my sister-in-law's husband, Jim: Thank each of you for all of your love, encouragement, patience, and support. You guys are the greatest cheerleading squad one could ever hope to have on the sidelines. Your faith and confidence in my success are the warm wind in sails, pushing me along on the open sea of opportunity.

***

To Strive, To Seek, To Find, and Not To Yield - Tennyson

Contents

INTRODUCTION

When we talk about generations, the myths are just as important as the general truths. These myths are made powerful because of how they shape the way we look at generations. They form the spaces or gaps in understanding between generational cohorts.

It helps to identify the gaps that exist between the five generations that make up our workforce. This isn't to point out how they are different, but instead to find common ground between the generations. As a premise of this book, with the right type of leadership and investment, organizations can attract, engage, and retain talent of any generation. If we focus on the commonalities and synergies between employees instead of their differences, we can arrive at a place where all employees of all generations can thrive.

THE FIVE GENERATIONS TARGETED BY THIS BOOK

TRADITIONALISTS (1)

Also known as the veterans or silent generation. For the purposes of research and this book, this generation was born between 1925 and 1945.

Events that shaped this generation:

- The Lindbergh flight
- The Lindbergh baby being kidnapped
- The stock market crash
- The Great Depression
- FDR
- The New Deal
- Start of Social Security
- Hitler invading Austria
- Pearl Harbor
- D-Day
- Victory Day
- The Korean War

The values and characteristics of this generation:

- Patriotism
- Loyalty
- Civic pride
- Respect for authority.

Myths about this generation:

- They have more accidents and are sick more
- They can't learn technology and aren't even interested in it
- They aren't as bright as their younger counterparts

They see themselves as keepers of wisdom and value loyalty, hard work, the chain of command, conformity, and sacrifice. Though they're the smallest generation of the four, they're the richest retirees and most charitable generation. They work well beyond retirement age, and the men have had a pretty smooth career compared to younger generations that follow. However, the exodus of Traditionalists obviously is accelerating, and we are soon approaching when it will be just Boomers, Gen X, Millennials and the new kids on the block, Gen Z.

BABY BOOMERS (2)

They believe in social activism first and values second. For this book, this generation was born between 1945 and 1964.

Events that shaped this generation:

- Rosa Parks
- Civil Rights
- First nuclear power plant
- Civil rights act
- Birth control
- JFK elected
- Cuban missile crisis
- Orbiting of the earth by John Glenn
- Moon landing
- Martin Luther King, Jr.'s I have a dream speech and his assassination
- Kennedy assassinations
- Woodstock

The values and characteristics of this generation:

- Optimism
- Opportunity
- Progress
- Passionate about participation, teams, and growth-oriented activities
- Involved in their community
- A strong sense of ownership

Myths about this generation:

- Baby Boomers are on their way out
- They always had it easy and are assured a comfortable retirement
- They've quit learning
- They define everyone else as the problem
- They're career driven workaholics, they're not driven to retire
- They're not IT savvy and don't embrace technology
- They're running the financial systems of the world to suit themselves

They believe in earning your position and adhere to rules and processes. They seem to live to work and want status symbols. Feedback isn't as important as it is to the generations that follow. Baby Boomers work hard and make 50 and 60 look like the new 30 or 40.

GEN X (3)

My generation was born between 1965 and 1980. The events that shaped our generation:

- Women's liberation
- Arab terrorists at Munich Olympics
- Watergate
- Energy crisis
- The Challenger disaster
- Jonestown
- Three Mile Island
- U.S. layoffs
- Iran hostages
- John Lennon's death
- Terrorists blowing up flights
- Exxon Valdez
- Fall of Berlin Wall
- Operation Desert Storm

Operation Desert Storm is also personal to me, an Operation Desert Storm veteran. I entered the U.S. Navy in 1990 during Operation Desert Shield which while I was in bootcamp became Operation Desert Storm. So not just an event that shaped my generation, but one that shaped me personally as a man, as a professional, and really has had a major impact on my becoming the person I'm today.

The values they bring are:

- Think globally and embrace diversity
- Technology literate
- Fun and informal
- Self-reliant
- Pragmatic

- Value financial security
- Better educated
- Clear about balance in our lives
- Value control over our time

Myths about this generation:

- We're very materialistic
- We're whiners
- We have a "you owe me" attitude
- We're not willing to work hard and want to live on easy street
- We won't attend meetings after 5
- We're flaky and disloyal
- We're slackers and lazy
- We ignore our careers
- We watch a lot of TV and play a lot of video games

Gen X is seen as the most entrepreneurial generation because we have been asked to go it alone quite early in our lives. We like to figure things out on our own. We invest in people, not necessarily organizations. We're constantly learning, and are adept and comfortable with change.

My generation is loyal to self, realizing that the only thing we can control is our own careers and our own ability to decide where we spend our time. We see ourselves as working to live, not living to work. That is very different from Baby Boomers, who spend their lives working hard so they can look forward to retirement.

Speaking as a Gen Xer, I really try to live each day as if it were my last, by doing what I want to do … and how I want to do it.

MILLENNIALS (4)

Also known as Gen Y, they're born between 1980 and 1995.

Events that shaped this generation:

- The Oklahoma bombings
- Columbine school shootings
- The Clinton and Lewinski scandal
- 9/11

The values and characteristics of this generation:

- Sociable
- Street smarts
- Hip and fun
- They believe in inclusion and group activities
- Work-life balance
- Confident
- Deep love of parents
- They respect authority but are also comfortable with informal authority
- They focus on meaningful work rather than money
- Digital natives
- They're driven by morality and compassion toward others

Myths about this generation:

- They have no work ethic
- They're spoiled
- They're entitled
- Little respect for older generations
- Spend money like water
- They want the top job on day one
- They want to be left alone
- Money and traditional benefits don't matter
- They're high maintenance

They came from a home where both mom and dad focused on the child. Mom and dad set up things for them to do and the kids then followed that schedule. These "helicopter parents" never really left their side. This is the generation where in sports and competitions, everyone wins, everyone gets a trophy. It's more about playing nice than winning. This is very different from the other generations, and they see that as challenging to develop drive, desire, and discipline in the workforce. Millennials grew up with generally more affluent parents who have disposable income and were able to spend that money on their childhood.

They believe in a return to traditional values with a little bit of a twist. This is a direct link to the Traditionalists, and very interesting how the differences can, with a closer look, unite rather than divide through similarities.

This is the generation that believes they should change jobs every few years, which has kind of bled over from Gen X. The idea of staying at a company for 10 years once upon a time was seen as a short timer. Now with this generation having such an influence on the workforce, so changing jobs every three years has become the norm.

GENERATION Z (5)

Also known as the iGeneration, or Homelanders, they were born after 1996.

Events that shaped this generation:

- The economic recession of 2008
- Mobile technology
- Global terrorism
- Internet of things
- Same-sex marriage

The values and characteristics of this generation:

- Determined
- Compassionate
- They in crowdsourcing and learning and new experiences via the Internet
- Socially aware
- Confident
- Spontaneous and adventuresome
- More educated than previous generations at an earlier age
- They are generally more risk-averse as a cohort
- The most ethnically diverse generation
- They're more prone to depression brought on by societal expectations

Myths about this generation:

- They're high maintenance
- They constantly seek feedback
- They're entitled
- They're not concerned about their future
- They cannot hold an in-person conversation
- Money and traditional benefits don't matter

Engaging Millennials and Gen Z

The most common complaint I hear about both generations is that they want to rise through the ranks of the organization too quickly, that they don't have realistic expectations for their career and that they need to temper their enthusiasm. And to that, I ask, "Is that really a bad thing?" Don't we want our employees to be enthusiastic and engaged? All of the research—and my own experience—clearly points to the paradigm of engaged employees are more productive. So why don't we figure out ways to harness and unleash that energy and enthusiasm and put it to good use? I'm sure there are a few over-exuberant types that need to be sat down and given some advice regarding their expectations. But the overwhelming majority of Millennials are just looking to be challenged and to be given an opportunity to do something meaningful. They want to learn, so let them, give them the experiences they need to keep them motivated and engaged.

The challenge is that most organizations don't do much to promote and capture such engagement from the outset. The organization goes out of its way to recruit the 'best and brightest.' But when they come into the office on day one, they go through death by PowerPoint orientation, they're shown where the bathrooms are, where the cafeteria is located, and then ushered to the cubicle where they'll be spending 40-50 hours a week for the next five years. The excitement of a new position quickly fades and turns into the stark reality that work life is much different than their days in college. Not all organizations are this bad, but even the good ones could do better.

If you are concerned, that these two younger generations want to jump to the next job too quickly, then explain to them how expanding the scope of their current role and taking on new challenges creates an opportunity for them. Growing in a role with their current organization is just as important, if not more important, than jumping ship to the next employer. The trick here for the organization is to create the leeway for roles to be easily expanded and built upon. Roles that are too rigid or too tightly defined won't offer employees the opportunity to expand his/her scope. Millennials want to know that they have options and a choice of career opportunities ahead of them in an organization. And your even younger Gen Z employees want to know what plans you as their manager have for them to prove themselves. You need to help them see that options exist and that their learning and further development will happen in a multitude of ways.

Organizations that retain younger talent do so by creating opportunities for all employees to learn through others and should encourage employees to seek out mentors, coaches, and sponsors to help them move their careers forward. The traditional way to do this is to set up mentoring circles, and have older employees take the younger employees under their wings. This works and is a nice way to transfer organizational knowledge, but it's not sufficient by itself. Employees should be encouraged to seek perspectives from outside of their function and from outside of their organization. In today's world of work, connecting the dots between how work gets done and what can be transferred from one discipline to another is an important and critical quality to have. The best in class organizations that we have seen create and manufacture opportunities for employees to grow their networks, both internally and externally.

Millennials now make up the majority of the workforce and are shaping the way that we think about and organize our work, and they'll continue to transform our people practices. It's time to embrace what they bring with them and understand what will engage them across the employee lifecycle. It's not enough to only focus on the recruiting; the process needs to extend through the employee lifecycle. And learning needs to be more than just a one-stop destination, it's a journey that spans multiple fronts. Successful organizations recognize this and establish principles and practices that complement that understanding.

Integrating Millennials and Nexters

Create a culture where all generations value and respect one another's capabilities to accomplish a task, whether it's building a new product, streamlining a process, closing a deal or brokering a sale.

The angst that currently exists with leaders of organizations about multiple generation workforces comes from a place of fear and misunderstanding. The challenge, in many cases, is ignoring a host of labels for all generations, ranging from the obnoxious to the sublime. The truth, as is usually the case, lies somewhere in between. Unfortunately, any time labels are ascribed to a generation, we in effect prime the mindset of others to automatically assume them to be true. So when you hear things like, 'the younger generation just doesn't get it, they just want to be the boss today, and they don't care for experience,' it's fair to question their motivations as they enter the workforce. When you hear it enough times, it eventually becomes the truth for you.

Knowingly or unknowingly, if you're in a position to 'make it right' there's a good chance that you're going to do so, at any cost.

Millennials especially have been given some of the most pejorative labels. But they also hold misconceptions about their older peers, which contributes to each believing that the other label is accurate. The thought that 'they aren't tech savvy, or aren't up to speed on what's new and hot,' has implications for how they may interact with one another. The assumption being that the older coworker has not taken the time to stay current or to stay close to the shifts underway in technology, business, customer service, mass customization, automation, etc. There may even be a devaluing of experience and the lessons that are learned along the way. What underlies this notion, is the thought that the experience, although valuable, is too outdated to be relevant in today's world and that the lessons learned aren't transferable across time, industry or market. On the flip side, the older think, the younger are 'too smart for their own good... they've had it easy.'

Assumptions that are made based on predetermined generalizations are dangerous to the entire fabric of an organization's culture. They can readily undermine the stability of the group and create a culture of inclusion and exclusion—of divisiveness—that ultimately has a bottom-line impact on the business. Retention, engagement, and productivity all suffer as a result of a culture where such a division is the norm. Luckily, the solutions to care for this issue aren't all that difficult. However, they do take time, energy and a consistent focus. If done correctly, over time the solutions become habitual and will lead to an enhanced experience across the board for all generations. Work is most productive when the forces at play are collaborative, multi-disciplined and have a variety of experiences. The idea that everyone adds value to a team and to a project is what becomes crucial when thinking about leading a multigenerational workforce.

First and foremost is to recognize that we all make assumptions and whether you want to admit it or not, they impact the way that we think and act. Not all biases are inherently dangerous, although they can certainly become so if we allow them. What we need people to recognize is that they have a bias and if they're willing, they can work through them and not enable it to cloud their judgment. If we hold onto them, we ultimately create a one-dimensional view of that individual. This misrepresentation of the individual can lead to us missing out on some other qualities, skills, and behaviors that the person possesses. We need to move beyond those thoughts and that mindset. Most people get stuck at this step, although it's not difficult to overcome. It requires that we retrain ourselves to press pause and react less quickly to what's around us.

We can reason and reject our initial impulses and give ourselves time to make judgments and accurate assumptions about individuals. The reality is that we need to pause, take a few breaths and think about it for a few more seconds (yes, seconds, it doesn't have to take forever). After we pause and allow ourselves a moment to reflect before moving forward with our interaction, it's time to engage. During the engagement, it's still critical to recognize that you have biases that can impact your assumptions about someone else and how that may influence the conversation. You can use a probing technique during your conversation to help you understand more about the individual. Avoid any questions with the word 'why.' It will only come across as negative. Instead, you should use questions and statements, such as, "tell me more... how do you feel about that? ... what I hear you say is...."

Using open-ended questions allows the conversation to move forward in a more structured way. It also gives you some time to think and reflect on what you're hearing from the individual. This technique will help you foster the development of a more integrated and inclusive workplace. If you want to integrate multiple generations into your workforce, you need to create an environment of mutual respect and ease of communication. Employees should seek to understand one another and look for patterns that utilize the power of the individuals' similarities or common bond and uniqueness.

There are processes you can put in place to enable these types of interactions. And it doesn't have to be a training event, which too easily can become a check the box activity. It needs to live beyond the classroom, and it should be embedded in your culture. If you need training to make people aware of how to interact, that's a place to start, but it's not enough. You can structure your work teams to care for cross-collaboration between generations. You can set up mentoring circles, host reverse-mentoring sessions, and put project teams together that represent different skill sets from across generations. The process for integrating multiple generations into a work environment doesn't have to be complex or disrupt the way work gets done, but it does take time and some effort. It is about recognizing and rewarding the unique attributes that everyone brings to the table. It's about rejecting misplaced, preconceived notions about the 'other' and about opening up and respecting what everyone brings to the table. Take the time to orient your employees on how they can learn to work across generations, demonstrate the value that they all bring to the organization.

***

Now let's talk about the challenges. What is this gap we're minding? More importantly, how do we mind this generational gap, so we get business results? I see many organizations that I've worked with, and senior leaders that I've talked to, struggle to work through how to get business results from an organization made up of many different generations that want different things.

There are all these conversations on the Internet and at different conferences about employee engagement and what is needed to hold onto Millennial, and now Gen Z talent. I wanted to boil it down simply and talk about what we can do to help organizations and leaders focus on minding the gap.

Today, so many organizations are flatter and freer of hierarchy. Employees that were once segregated by age and position are now working more closely together. The flatter the organization, the more it takes to effectively execute a business strategy. The differences in the ages of employees working side by side will only widen in the coming years. According to the National Association of Colleges and Employers (NACE), companies expect to hire a greater number of younger college graduates than in the previous four years.

Members of each generation bring distinct sets of values and behaviors in the workplace. These five generations come to work with different expectations, assumptions, priorities, and approaches to work and communication, which will either help or hinder organizations. Not only is the workforce changing generationally, so too is our customer base. Much more than ever, the organizations that do well ... will be those that mirror the community they serve. Success will come to those organizations that realize this and take action early on to serve their diverse client base.

When we appropriately manage the idea of this generational challenge to really create opportunities for collaboration and synergy of the different generations, it gives the organization a competitive edge. I will later dive more into what motivates employees at work and home. Why do they come to work? What's it that they're seeking? What does work-life balance mean to them? What's it that employers need to be prepared to ask of them? More importantly, what do they need to do that isn't asked of them? There is a lot of informal wanting and needing that will go on between the generations, and if employers are not up to the challenge of connecting the wanting to the being willing, they'll miss the opportunity to really get business results.

Today, Gen Xers, Millennials, and Gen Z together make up 60% of American workers. Baby Boomers make up a smaller 31%, but still, hold the lion's share of leadership positions. If they don't understand the younger generations or refuse to change their thinking, this then becomes a business challenge.

Traditionalists might be the most experienced. But these hard-working members of the part-time or gig economy workforce are enjoying life, and are mostly working to keep from being bored, or to stay physically active.

Gen X is a generation of fewer people, and here to there is a shrinking pool of prime-age workers. Many Gen Xers become entrepreneurs, and there's going to be a generational gap of leaders. As a rough estimate, there are 78 million Baby Boomers. And most positions of leadership are held by these members of this generation. But the next generation, Gen X is only about 50 million. Of that generation, many have decided that corporate America and the traditional notion of the "American dream" are dead. Currently, two Gen X workers exit the traditional workforce for every one Millennial entering. The demand for bright and talented Gen X leaders will increase, creating a leadership deficit.

Millennial employees will have to develop faster, which means they will be put in leadership roles long before they should be there, or feel that they are ready ... and without the experiences they need. This will be a challenge for leaders and organizations. Another challenge is competition for seasoned, experienced decision makers. There's a recruiting war coming. Top Gen X talent will have options and will be able to move into positions of leadership and influence within organizations.

***

Companies are scrambling to implement more aggressive retention measures and recruit more competitively than ever. They need to meet the challenges presented by these evolutionary changes in the workforce. For the longest time, it's been something that was seen as a nuisance, as something quirky about organizations with both younger and older employees working together. Now we're in a place where more and more leaders and organizations are realizing it's a serious challenge to them. It opens the door for talent mobility. How do we look at the workforce that we have, measure it against the one that we need, and look at how to close the gap? How do we look at getting the right people, in the right roles, at the right time, with the right skills, for the right cost?

Every business strategy is dependent on having top talent within the organization to execute the strategy. What if you can't get that? What if you have people from different generations working together that can't understand each other? Or worse, what if you have leaders who don't understand the different generations in the workforce? Well, the need to answer these questions was my impetus for the writing this book you are currently reading.

***

The first chapter of this book is about how to help employees feel welcome. I'll share my ideas on how we can better use workforce planning and informed talent management to build a culture of inclusion.

Chapter two is about how to make employees feel valued. Can we take a more contemporary look at employee engagement to benefit all generational cohorts? How are we developing our people for the future? How can we create an organization for our employees where they don't feel like a means to an end but instead realize that they are critical to organizational success?

We'll move then to chapter three, where I will offer the thinking that leaders in organization own helping employees to feel free to be their authentic self at work. I tell my clients all the time that retention issues start with poor employee engagement. No one can truly be engaged when spending all of their energy trying to be on their best behavior in a place where they cannot be themselves.

Chapter four is about making changes to your organization's internal workforce. We'll talk about how to get employees to contribute their best. That means talent deployment. How do we put people in the right role at the right time? That goes back to one of the greatest business books that have ever been written, about getting the right people on the bus. Even more is getting them in the right seat. How do you put someone in a seat they're not ready for? What happens when the seat was made for and by another generation?

Chapter five we'll discuss how to help leaders bridge the generational gap. How do we work with these different generations? We'll talk about what each generation comes to the workplace wanting. We'll spend some time in that chapter talking about setting expectations, the different motivations of the generations, and aspects of development. Also, important topics are feedback and coaching. The presence of feedback helps to round out the learning of how to be an effective leader. We'll talk about aspirations, recognition, and other aspects for each generation that round out what our employees of any generation come to the office expecting to find.

The last chapter, chapter six, we'll outline how to go about getting business results. How do we pull it all together? Now more than ever, this book is one that is prime reading to help business leaders discover things they can do differently, and walk away having an action plan. This alone will help them bridge the gap that, for some, is keeping them from being the company they need to be tomorrow. And we mover forward by understanding the company and workforce of today.

GETTING GENERATIONAL

If managing a multigenerational workforce isn't something that you've been thinking about, it's time to start.

There are currently forty million Millennials in the workforce, by 2020 there will be more of them than Boomers in the workplace. By 2025 they will account for fifty percent of the workforce, and by 2030 three out of every four workers worldwide will be of the Millennial generation. This great generational shift is happening right beneath your feet, and it's shaking the workforce at the core. But, let's be clear, this tectonic shift is more than just the generational upheaval that's occurring. It's also about the changing nature of how we work, the tools that we use to get that work done, the increasingly globalized environment in which we operate, and the pace of everything and everyone around us. It's time that we start thinking about what we need to do to create an engaged and committed workforce across all generations.

Much has been written over the last 10 years about the Millennial generation, including scathing articles about them being lazy, self-centered, myopic and needy. I think these accusations are massively unfair and a generalization across an entire generation that is still amid development. Are there Millennials that are lazy, entitled and self-centered? Absolutely, but so are some people in all other generations that have come before us. It's wrong to assume that because you have a Millennial on your team, they are going to live up to the label.

A famous study done by Ray Rist in 1970 looked at how social class became a predictor for placement in the classroom. The middle-class students made up the 'fast-track' while lower-income students fell into the pack of slow learners. The implications for this are enormous, and such labels are dangerous. Priming leaders with this notion that the next generation is vastly different from any other based on patterns of behaviors is misguided at best.

My first piece of advice when it comes to managing a multigenerational workforce is to avoid making assumptions or casting broad allegations about any generation. Manage your people as individuals, not as a component of a larger organism. It's unfair and unjust to do so. Look at the long-tail phenomenon that's taking hold in organizations like Amazon and Netflix. It's no longer enough to offer one type of service to your customers, based on an assessment of them in their entirety; individualization is real. Customization is important, in today's business environment, and determines how we package products and services. So why is it that when it comes to management and leadership, we assume that we can create one-size fits all systems for our workforce? If you choose to manage all your people the same way, you're doomed. This isn't about the Millennials being different than any other generation; it's actually about individuals being unique from one another.

There are some fundamental differences in the milieu in which Millennials were raised. The dates are subject to debate, but let's assume we mean the period of 1980-1995 when we talk about Millennials. They were born alongside the Internet, cell phones, video games and expanding globalization. From a historical context, they've seen the fall of the Berlin Wall, the Soviet Union crumble, the dot.com bubble burst, the 9/11 terror attacks, wars in Iraq and Afghanistan and the Great Recession. They've lived through an unprecedented time when ideas go viral overnight, and goods and services deliver to customers and clients at a pace the world has never experienced before. The context in which they were raised is vastly different than that of their predecessors, but each generation has a story to tell: from the World Wars to Hiroshima and Nagasaki, to the Space Race and Sputnik, men on the moon and Vietnam. We're not immune to the context—the events of the times—in which members of different generations were raised. It certainly plays a role in shaping our perceptions and opinions, which impact our actions. But to say that each of us responds in kind, to what we collectively experience, is where everything falls apart for me. We are each unique and deserve to be treated as such. We're not one and the same. If you choose to lead your workforce this way, you're setting yourself up for a disengaged and disenchanted workplace.

The question then becomes how to lead a multigenerational workforce, with a seismic change currently underway. It's simple. This isn't rocket science. To lead, you must start to understand what motivates and drives your employees. Define a purpose for them, build paths of opportunity and create a space that allows for all people, across all generations to contribute their thoughts and skillsets.

If you read what has been said about Millennials, leaders and managers are told about giving them opportunities, providing them with training, and warning them of the dangers of social media. This is all valid points, to a degree; again, they're platitudes and generalizations. Not every one of your Millennials is looking to rule the world or the company. Most, however—and this is important, perhaps even crucial—want to make a difference in some fundamental way. Don't we all? Another criticism leveled is that Millennials think they can take the top spot in any organizations, at any time. If this is the case, it means they're ambitious, and I'd ask, is that such a bad thing? The real question—fear—at the heart of this is whether many, or any, of them, represent or desire a subversion of authority and portray a lack of respect for tradition and process that can weaken or damage the organization.

Again, those are massive generalizations. But if this is a concern, shouldn't we look at the way society has eroded the hierarchical norms, 'traditional values' and respect. It wasn't the Millennials responsible for driving this, they were too busy playing video games to notice what was going on. It was their parents and others before them. That said, even if

16

this is indeed the case, why don't we harness what motivates them and find ways to channel it appropriately. Consider giving them a voice at the table, look for the means to incorporate their ideas. This is talent management at its simplest. Find the people who have the ambition, skills, and abilities, that are engaged and aspire to do more, and give them a chance. There are plenty of opportunities across any organization to let people experiment with new ideas or new initiatives.

Leading a multigenerational workforce doesn't have to be difficult. Millennials aren't some alien lifeform being introduced into organizations, but they are helping to change the way we think about work, engagement, and organizations. Tap into what they know, leverage their expertise with social media and technology. Let me be clear, they are one of many variables that are shaping the workforce today, and for tomorrow. External and environmental conditions, technology and globalization, are huge factors disrupting the 'traditional' notions of work and management. This is a good thing; we need to find ways to embrace it. Consider the Millennials ready, as ready as any other generation in your workforce, to do so. You need to find the right balance of engagement and purpose to lead them effectively. Start with treating them as individuals, then consider ways to let your people shine by giving them opportunities at the right time and at the right moment.

BUT WHAT ABOUT GEN Z?

Gen Z, also known as the iGeneration. This is the generation born after Millennials that is emerging as the next big shift in thinking according to market researchers, cultural observers, and trend forecasters. Generational study being more art than science, there is a considerable dispute about the definition of Gen Z. Demographers place it's beginning anywhere from the mid-'90s to the mid-2010s. Marketers and trend forecasters, however, who tend to slice generations into bite-sized units, often characterize this generation as a roughly 20-year span starting around 1996, making them between 3 to 23 years old at the time of this writing. (By that definition, Millennials were born between about 1980 and 1995, and are roughly 24 to 39 now.)

With the oldest members of this cohort just now coming out of college, these young professionals of today are primed to become the dominant youth influencers of tomorrow. And while it is easy to mock the efforts of marketers to shoehorn tens of millions of people into a generational archetype, à la the Baby Boomers, it is also clear that a 23-year-old in 2019 really does inhabit a substantially different world than one of 2009. Millennials, after all, were raised during the boom times and relative peace of the 1990s, only to see their sunny world dashed by the Sept. 11 attacks and two economic crashes, in 2000 and 2008. Theirs is a story of innocence lost. Generation Z, by contrast, has had its eyes open from the beginning, coming along in the aftermath of those cataclysms in the era of the war on terror and the Great Recession.

Gen Z takes in information instantaneously and loses interest almost equally as fast. And the parents of these teenagers play an influential role in shaping their collective outlook. Millennials, who are often painted, however unfairly, as narcissistic brats who expect the boss to fetch them coffee, were mainly raised by Baby Boomers, who, according to many, are the most iconoclastic, self-absorbed and grandiose generation in history.

By contrast, Generation Z is the product of Generation X, my generation that came of age in the post-Watergate, post-Vietnam funk of the 1970s, when horizons seemed limited. "As the former latchkey kids, we grew up watching MTV, and slasher movies, have tried to give our children the safe, secure childhood that they never had," said Neil Howe, an economist and the co-author of more than a dozen books about American generations. Part of our obsession with safety for our children is due to the hard times that both Generation Z members and we, as their parents, experienced during our formative years. Growing up in a time of hardship, global conflict, and economic troubles have affected their future.

As GENERATIONS AGE

My own research on this critical topic has led to a series of successful strategies to implement to fully engage each generation in your organization. We'll first look at recruiting as a tool to bring diversity into your organization and the impact that it has on your customers and employee base. Next, we'll look at how development initiatives can be used to spark engagement and drive knowledge management in your organization. Lastly, we'll talk about how to handle off-boarding and retiring employees leaving the organization. Combined, these three strategies create a system that recognizes and takes advantage of, the strengths of each generation while integrally creating spaces where they can work more productively and learn from one another.

According to the *Economist* (see *March of the Greybeards),* there is a growing trend of employers hiring older unemployed or underemployed employees in Britain. In 2020, it's expected that almost one-third of the workforce will be over 50. Employers aren't backing away from the aging workforce, but rather they are intentionally embracing them as a core component of the hiring and recruiting strategy. Many organizations are retraining their existing workforce to become upskilled in new technologies, new tools and new ways of work, while others, like Barclay's, are introducing programs known as 'bold apprenticeships' where they are actively reaching out to and recruiting older workers. This strategy recognizes the changing demographics and attempts to harness the collective knowledge of older workers. True, older workers may not have the same motivations of their younger counterparts, but they have the value of experience and with that comes an understanding of where to apply their energies and when it's appropriate to take short cuts. In a nutshell, they're more cunning than their younger counterparts.

Building a workforce with intentionality starts with recruiting. Creating a space for older workers to bring in their veteran set of skills and knowledge establishes a particular culture in an organization and *should* create a ripple effect on the younger generations (for those willing to pay attention to and understand the value that knowledge and experience brings). Recruiting older generations also mirrors the population's demographics. It's true that customers prefer to work with people they can relate to, and for the older generations, this holds true more than ever. There are two facets to consider when thinking about recruiting older workers for your organization. You can hire directly from the outside, understanding that it's likely a shorter-term investment strategy, or you can build programs to retrain your existing, aging, workforce to keep them fresh in their skillsets. It's the old, buy vs. build question. Are the skills that you're asking your employees to acquire attainable in a reasonable time frame or are they more readily available outside of the organization? The answer probably lies somewhere in between.

Development in most organizations varies widely, from functionally specific learning to leadership programs. Most target an audience with a very exact intent and purpose. What we've learned over the years is that there is great power in the hidden curriculum. What happens between the classes, in the hallways and at the tables in the classroom while on break, can sometimes be just as powerful if not, stronger than the actual learning itself. When designing and building development programs for multiple generations, it's important to create spaces where people can interact and learn from one another above and beyond the standard learning format. Building a network for learners after the session is over has a profound impact on how work gets done within your organization. Employees who have attended our programs in the past, always comment on the relationships that they've built and the lasting network forged through this experience.

If you're recruiting and bringing older generations into your workforce, do so purposefully. You should put them into positions where others can learn from them while they, in turn, learn from others about the organization's culture and protocols. If you bring them in because of the value of their experience, make sure you allow them to share that experience.

The final piece of the strategy for managing the workforce is to understand that even though it's a short-term investment, the long play is to create systems and practices that enable the organization to capture knowledge and share it broadly for years to come. If you don't have a knowledge management system in place, you're letting years of experience, know-how, and intellectual property walk out of your doors every day. The technologies that exist today to build an integrated knowledge management system are easy to use, easy to implement and fairly inexpensive. Utilize them to create mentoring opportunities and shadowing experiences so that your younger employees have the chance to learn directly from employees who are set to leave the organization. Doing so enables employees to learn and grow from one another, and for those employees that are about to retire and move on, it gives them a chance to share their legacy with the next in line.

Developing a strategy on how to deal with an aging workforce is just as important as understanding how to best deal with bringing Millennials and Gen Z employees into your organization. It requires a strategic viewpoint and planning.

CHAPTER 1

HOW TO MAKE EMPLOYEES FEEL WELCOME

How do we build a workforce where employees can feel they're part of an organization that is in line with their values and desires? Any business strategy has a human component. Managers and leaders need to engage employees in a way that makes them stay. That helps them to contribute and provide good customer service, which leads to happy and loyal customers, which means a successful and profitable business. When you think about trying to get business results from a multigenerational workforce, it starts with making sure employees are engaged.

Talent practices and inclusive talent management are really important to sustain a multigenerational workforce because it addresses vital strategic and organizational issues. Productivity improvement is the number one driver for improved talent management practices. Leaders invest in technology and improved processes, but those processes only get them so far, because you have to deal with the people within the organization. If you look at moving forward with people, people are always seen as a cost. When you think of the cost of having employees in the organization, you want the best out of those employees.

PLAN TODAY FOR THE WORKFORCE YOU NEED TOMORROW

It's important for organizations to not only do their hiring for today. Does the person I hire have skills that are not only helpful now, but also helpful as we move into the future? I don't know of many organizations that don't expect to change. One of the reasons why I'm writing this book is to help organizations realize that when they're hiring someone in, they're hiring them in for more than just today. Even if those employees don't plan to stay in that organization long. Risk can be mitigated with proper preparation, and the organization can respond more agilely to any situation that might challenge its ability to meet its business strategy.

***

We have to think about organizational strategy and what we're trying to achieve. If we don't know where we're going, how will we know if we have the right people in place to assist us? Do we have the right people,

21

in the right role, with the right skills, at the right time, at the right cost? If we can't answer yes to any of those five questions, it means we don't have the workforce in place to drive the organization.

Sometimes Human Resources (HR) gets a bad name because it doesn't help the organization have the talent it needs, but not having a plan can limit the ability of HR to be a strategic partner. If we can keep in mind as we move forward that everything starts with business strategy and that everything is tied to that, it allows us to make informed decisions about minding the gap within the organization. Our workforce today will be made up of different generations, with different needs. We have to understand who's working for us and help them feel welcome, so they're engaged.

Everything depends on where the business wants to go. The strategy in place should be one that allows your organization to set yourself apart from others. How are you going to be different? Where are you going? How are you trying to win? How are you fighting to stay number one or working hard to be number one? As I've seen with most organizations that I've consulted, most top tier organizations are either number one, or number two fighting to be number one. Those that are successful are so because they realize the people, really the people, are the difference between them and the other organizations with which they're competing.

***

How do we bring people in? The business strategy should be set, so we know what kind of talent we need; the specific pieces and roles critical for achieving the business strategy. What are the skills needed by people in those roles? Take a good hard look at the organization and ask, do we have the right people in the right role at the right time? If not, then what's getting in the way? Is it work styles or work preferences of different generations? Is it the leadership that isn't working to bring out the best in people? If the strategy is set up so that people of all different generations don't have a line of sight to how their role helps execute the strategy, we as leaders need to work on that. We need to be equipping our leaders to answer those questions.

***

Many people think talent acquisition and recruiting are synonymous, but talent acquisition is much broader. Recruiting is putting a fishing pole in the water and hope to have a fish bite on what you're advertising. Talent acquisition is much different, where you go out and find the talent that you need. That's one of the things that makes it different if you as an organization are looking to bring in top talent of the different generations, but your recruiters are of the mindset of only their generation is the best prepared. Are they committed to finding top talent that happens to be ethnically diverse, gender diverse, and multigenerational? Without that commitment, you won't be able to find the top talent you need. Top talent within your organization's workforce allows you to act, not just react.

As mentioned in the introduction, the workforce is getting younger. How we recruit and attract talent is different. Now we use more social media and crowdsourcing. Recruiting in organizations is separate from other parts and because of that, recruiters are on the front line and understand more than anyone that generational diversity exists, and that appealing to generations will look and sound different from each other.

Now companies, more than ever, are looking to assess cultural and behavioral fit as well as technical skills. Baby Boomer hiring managers want to make sure whoever they hire will fit in with the culture that they have spent time building or will fit in with a culture they now lead. There's nothing wrong with wanting to go work and work with people you like, and whom you get along with, but if that is more important than bringing in top talent, then we have to look and understand why. Is there one leader that is only hiring Baby Boomers? Why is there one leader only hiring Millennials? What's the perceived value by only hiring out of one generation? What are the biases that exist that can be mitigated by understanding the generations? When someone is brought into an organization, never at any other moment than when they first start will you have the level of engagement and opportunity to let someone feel welcome.

A Message to Managers

The workplace is becoming increasingly diverse, with many companies making efforts to employ workers from different backgrounds. For the first time, the United States has five generations of people still working alongside one another. The five current generations in the workplace are Traditionalists, Baby Boomers, Generation X, Millennials, and Gen Z.

As work-life expectancy is expanding, many employees find themselves still employed at 75, extending the overlap between generations. Researchers have determined that each generation shares values, goals, and beliefs that define and differentiate them from other generations.

By 2025, many researchers suggest that Millennials will make up 50% of the U.S. Labor Force. The number of Millennials turning 35 daily is equal to the number of Baby Boomers retiring each day, roughly ten thousand. Baby Boomers staying in the organization have a long-lasting ripple effect on Millennials (and Generation X) workers. The numbers of employees alone is staggering, and managing the workforce while trying to attract, engage, and retain members of the youngest generation, Gen Z who is a differently motivated employee generation is daunting... but not impossible.

Generational diversity in the workplace may pose challenges for organizations. Specifically, the mix of generations in the workforce presents the greatest challenges for managers. However, these same challenges can also create opportunities. Employees create psychological contracts with their employers that reflect their values and attitudes toward work. These contracts are informal agreements between employees and employers. Thus, it is imperative for leaders to understand each of these generations, and to classify them by cohort. Once aligned by cohort, these generations can be classified based on shared goals, values, and beliefs that differentiate them from other generations.

Baby Boomers were born between 1946 and 1964. Many of the members of this cohort continue to work into their late 60s and early 70s. They are the largest generational cohort, accounting for more than 40% of the current workforce. Thus, they have had a significant impact on society and the modern workplace. Their core values include optimism, personal gratification, and growth. They grew up during a period of prosperity in the United States. Money, titles, and recognition motivate them. The Civil Rights movement, women's liberation, the Cuban Missile Crisis, the Vietnam War, Woodstock, and the invention of television define their lives.

Generation X was born between 1965 and 1980. Generation X represents approximately 34% of the current workforce. They are the children of compulsive workers from the previous generational cohort, which shapes their views about work, money, titles, and recognition.

Their core values include diversity, being technologically savvy, and informality. Their lives are defined by the AIDS epidemic and oil embargo.

Millennials were born between 1981 and 1995. This generation comprises about 20% of the workforce. They are the largest generational cohort to enter the workforce since the Baby Boomers. Their core values include optimism, civic duty, and confidence. Their lives are defined by times of significant transition: the Oklahoma City bombing and the terrorist attacks of September 11, 2001.

Gen Z was born on or after the year 1996. They are the most racially and ethnically diverse generational cohort. Their core values include fearlessness, boldness, and achievement. They have shown signs of being comfortable pursuing opportunities outside of the traditional workplace, including entrepreneurial ventures, and they are willing to take a personal risk if they believe they have more to gain. Rapid technological advances define their lives.

Managing this diverse workforce of cohorts is essential to organizational sustainability. A cohort is a group of individuals who are born during the same period and journey through life together. The cohort approach is effective when comparing the same age groups or over a specified period. Generational cohort theory indicates that generational differences impact the values, morals, and work ethic of employees. Experiences related to dates of birth and shared experiences shape a generation. Managers must understand these generational differences to develop strategies to motivate a multigenerational workforce.

There will soon be a set of revolutionary changes in organizations as workplaces and cultures transition from 'Boomer-centric' to 'Millennial centric'; meaning that central elements of organizational strategies include transformations that appeal to Millennials. Each generation has different life expectations and is motivated by different life stage circumstances. The idea of managing the cultural transition as concerns unique to Baby Boomers or Millennials is an issue in organizational culture. For example, Clark and Ghent described how decisions that targeted Baby Boomers' early retirement might achieve the objective of increasing Millennials and youth in the organization, but could also increase the loss of valuable organizational knowledge held by Baby Boomers.

Understanding what aspects of the organizational culture provoke responses from people that share common beliefs and ideas underlines the significance of being cognizant of signals. This certainly comes into play in knowledge transfer and mentoring. Workplace design can address concerns of knowledge transfer and mentoring from older employees (i.e., Baby Boomers) to younger employees (i.e., Millennials). Workplace design that includes a team-based approach where Millennials and Baby Boomers are paired together to encourage knowledge from older to younger employees could improve performance.

Baby Boomers hierarchical; job focused and highly motivated to climb the corporate ladder. They live to work and experience tension between the younger generations because they expect others to have the same work ethic.

The next two cohorts represent the younger members of the workforce. However, the members of these cohorts all have different opinions, beliefs, and values that differentiate them from one another. Members of the Generation X cohort are independent, entrepreneurial, cynical, and anti-hierarchy. They work to live and view the world with cynicism and distrust. The Millennial cohort strives for work/life balance, rapid career advancement, and international travel. Having grown up with the Internet, Millennials more technologically savvy than previous generational cohorts. They demonstrate negative attitudes toward older adults.

Baby Boomers express low opinions of younger generations. The workaholic generation views Millennials, and Gen Z employees as slackers with no work ethic. They also feel these generational cohorts lack experience and rely too heavily on technology. However, they have a favorable view of the Traditionalist cohort and view them as valuable members of the workforce with experience that they can learn from and use to gain a competitive advantage in the workplace.

The Generation X cohort believes that the Millennial and Gen Z cohorts lack sufficient work ethic. However, they acknowledge their ability to grasp quickly new concepts and skills. Generation X has a high opinion of Traditionalists, who they consider team players and role models. They can have an adversarial relationship with Baby Boomers, who they feel are too rigid and lack appropriate work-life balance. Furthermore, they view both Traditionalists and Baby Boomers as slow learners who struggle to adapt to new technology.

Millennials view the Baby Boomers positively, seeing them as disciplined and hard working. This generational cohort relates to Baby Boomers as both cohorts also ambitious, and career focused. This ambition causes conflict with the Generation X cohort who are more focused on achieving a work/life balance. Millennials view Gen Z positively and admire their Traditionalist-like civic-minded approach to the world and their Generation X/Millennial-like ability to quickly grasp new concepts.

Gen Z shares a similar civic-mindedness with the Traditionalist cohort as both generations grew up in a time of war and economic uncertainty. They come in conflict with Baby Boomers because Gen Z prefers to interact electronically more than personally while Baby Boomers prefer face-to-face interaction. They share a technological link with members of Generation X and Millennial cohorts but are by far the most technologically savvy, connected cohort. Employee perceptions can lead to disharmony and chaos among the members of the workforce. However, understanding these perceptions can narrow the gap between the members of the multigenerational workforce. Managers can utilize this information to motivate a multigenerational workforce.

Members of Generation X are comfortable with technology and are often early adopters of new technology due to the rise of the Internet and smartphone communications that occurred during their formative years. Millennials were exposed to computers, mobile phones, and tablets at an early age; therefore, Millennials are comfortable and connected with technology. Not to mention Generation Z who have grown up with technology as teacher, friend, and babysitter, all in the palm of their hands through various portable electronic devices. Managers must work harder to stay aware of which style (and method) of communication works best for each generational cohort.

The focus areas that positively or negatively influence organizational culture: values shaped by experiences, characteristics, and stereotypes, and generational expectations of the work environment. Generational differences are commonly accepted and primarily attributed to the collective experiences and events in the lives of each generation that shaped their values and beliefs.

It can be explained that generational cohort is a term that distinguishes a group of individuals of a specific time having a common reference to experiences and historical events based on their birthright. Multigenerational theory is based on that people from different generational cohorts may view situations differently based on their own reference points of experiences and historical events, which ultimately influences their impact on organizational culture.

Another subtlety to the values disparity, or the perception thereof, is how current technology has played a role in learning and everyday practices. An example is online processes that encourage risk-taking and learning from mistakes. Technology allows decisions to be made more quickly, with only minor penalties for errors and encourages risk-taking and experimentation—behavior that could flourish in a Millennial-dominated organizational culture. Multigenerational interaction influences organizational and generational culture, and the intermingling of different value systems can lead to conflict. Competing viewpoints, attitudes, and values are sources of multigenerational conflict with a potential impact on organizational bottom-lines.

Multigenerational worker interaction requires an understanding of workplace expectations established by organizational values and goals. Both Baby Boomer and Millennial cohorts are expected to adapt and follow cultural and value norms. Thus, value differences between Millennials and Baby Boomers will influence workplace processes to facilitate member negotiation. Nothing highlights the enormity of the transition between Millennials and Baby Boomers and their impact on organizational culture more than the sheer volume of Millennials entering the workforce while Baby Boomers are leaving the workplace.

Aspiring to be promoted into positions vacated by retiring Baby Boomers, Millennials are instead stuck waiting for their opportunity while working for Boomers in their current jobs. Also, Millennials' initial perception upon entering the workforce can be swayed by their peers, and this has a potential impact on their retention and interaction with Baby Boomers. Millennials grew up in an atmosphere in which questioning their parents was the norm; moreover, direct engagement with authority is a Millennial expectation as opposed to a traditional chain of command structures that can include layers between employees and managers. Millennials enter the workplace with expectations of open communication, a horizontal (not vertical) leadership structure, and limited degrees of separation between them and the ability to speak to managers. This generational expectation is different from most organizational cultural norms in a Baby Boomer-centric environment. Such generational differences in expectations are a source of conflict as these two generational cohorts intermingle and engage in one workplace environment.

Organizational culture is also impacted by leadership styles and the different approaches used by the organization. In most cases, how the workforce engages is heavily influenced by the highest platform of leadership in the organization setting the tone. Organizational values affect engagement by satisfying group affiliation needs and appealing positively to cerebral expectations of accomplishment. Organizational leaders that appreciate the generational differences between Baby Boomers and Millennials, and are capable of exploiting those differences in some practical and strategic manner, increase odds of achieving success in productivity and performance.

A study of fifty multi-national companies focused on workplace preferences among employed college graduate Millennials and highly talented Gen Xers. One of the main findings suggested that when it came to work-life balance, the expectation was similar, meaning that both Gen Xers and Millennials had the same hopes and the central delineation could be attributed to current life stage. Baby boomers and Millennials have different value systems that converge and influence the organizational culture. Developing organizational strategies and processes to promote the best possible situation for success includes engagement through leadership.

Millennial engagement is necessary to achieve organizational success. There are four best practices prescribed approaches to engage Millennials:

- Provide access to leadership and include Millennials perception of leadership;
- Be transparent and support open access to information;
- Build and encourage engagement mediums in the social sphere for online and offline activity; and
- Promote an environment that is conducive to Millennial involvement in solution building that can influence organizational strategy.

Each of the generational cohorts is motivated differently. Millennials have a keen understanding and reliance on technology and arrive at the workplace expecting technology to be an integral part of the environment. On the other hand, Gen X, as a cohort, can become comfortable with technology use but do not have the same reverence for it as Millennials. From this perspective, ensuring organizational technology and core business applications are current is not just a smart business decision, but also a motivating factor for Millennials. Technology perceived as relevant or up to date is viewed by Millennials as a reason to join an organization or stay on.

The action required to motivate Millennials and Gen Xers can take many forms and is a contributing factor to the complexity of this subject. Identifying and integrating motivation into the organizational culture requires close attention to the differences and similarities, regardless of their complexity and seeming contradictions.

Mentoring emerged as an essential factor in my experience with multigenerational organizations. Mentoring is a motivating factor for Baby Boomers and Millennials. Expectedly, Baby Boomers would be seen as natural mentors to Millennials. However, Millennials are also mentors when considering the use of new technology, suggesting that mentoring is the act of retaining top talent and nurturing new an emphasis on the relationship aspect of mentorship, along with mutual respect between mentor and the person being mentored, could build the skills of each party. Moreover, motivating and engaging the workforce is more effective when the generational gaps are identified and managed in both directions. Motivated and engaged employees reduce the tension of organizational culture evolution.

Acknowledging that generational cohorts exist in the workplace with inherently different values, have generational differences influenced by their experiences, and fit into different demographics. Implementing practices that promote a harmonious environment affords managers the greatest chance to ensure positive organizational culture change, particularly change that is neither Baby Boomer nor Millennial centric but cohort encompassing.

Ideally, managers should deploy engagement strategies that balance the needs of each cohort with the end goal being a positive influence on organizational culture. Engagement of Millennial and Gen Z employees is necessary to retain or recruit talented employees and provides a nurturing environment that brings them into the desired corporate culture. Likewise, managers must ensure Baby Boomers, and Gen Xers are engaged in such a way that retains their experience as leaders who currently carry the baton for morale and followership behavior within the organization. Achieving this state requires an awareness of the engagement needs and value systems of each cohort to implement a solution.

Managers must maintain a focus on the people within their organization. Employee engagement is the leading factor in the success or failure of an organization. The process of getting to know their employees and finding commonalities with them is a useful motivational tool. To motivate someone as an employee, you must get to know them as a person first. Managers should be encouraged and trained to use different techniques to establish connections with employees from different generation cohorts. Managers should also use multiple communication channels to connect with employees including meetings, emails, and teleconferencing.

Modern managers are tasked with motivating an increasingly diverse workforce. However, some managers lack strategies to drive a multigenerational workforce. Leaders at all levels must adjust their leadership style to improve teamwork and collaboration. Teamwork and collaboration skills are essential to gaining and maintaining a competitive advantage in business.

Research points to all individuals being motivated by the same general needs. However, people born around the same time have shared common life events that serve as a basis for attitudes and behaviors. Managers must identify strategies to increase teamwork among generational cohorts with different workplace values. Teamwork is a job characteristic valued by all employees, regardless of generational cohorts. Team building could be used to help employees understand each other's generational work ethics. Effective managers use generational differences to enhance teamwork and increase collaboration.

Multigenerational teams are assets to an organization as each member brings unique strengths, viewpoints, and skills that enhance productivity, creativity, and collaboration. Managers must be aware of generational differences and cultivate an environment conducive to the successful collaboration of employees from a multigenerational workforce. Collaborating with employees on new policies and procedures before implementation could help with acceptance across the workforce. There is profound importance in including employees in the decision making whenever possible. Doing so is vital as a way to include employees so that they do not begin to feel excluded, which poses significant threats to motivation and collaboration. This goes a long way to make everyone feel included while paying attention to their unique attributes and skills.

Leaders of large and small organizations experience challenges motivating a workforce composed of five generations. Thus, these challenges require managers to seek new ideas for motivating a multigenerational workforce. Similarities exist between the members of the generations. Managers must understand the differences and similarities between the generational cohorts.

Management can use strategies that maximize these similarities while minimizing differences. Three recommended strategies for leaders are: (a) adaptive work schedules, (b) increased knowledge sharing, and (c) innovative management styles. Managers should provide options like telework for employees to improve the productivity of the multigenerational workforce. Knowledge sharing among older and younger employees fosters teamwork and maximizes the performance of the workforce. Technology should be used as a tool to enhance knowledge sharing. Leaders must adjust their leadership styles to adapt to the ways the members of the different generational cohorts think, learn, and respond.

Generation X and the Baby Boomers have significantly different values for public recognition and career goals. Gen X placed a higher value on self-directed career advancement and relied less on the organization for career growth, while the results from the Baby Boomers showed just the opposite: The Baby Boomers seek and expect recognition and promotional opportunities from the company.

A significant difference exists in organizational loyalty between Baby Boomers and Gen X employees. The Baby Boomers are on average much more committed to the company. Generation X employees are more committed than other generations to career security than to the organizations for which they work. Many have concluded that Baby Boomer employees "live to work" while Generation X employees "work to live."

Differences between Boomer and Gen Xers employees result in conflict when working together. These differences included a higher team orientation and reward orientation for the Baby Boomers while the Generation X employees were found to be more independent and high technology oriented. These differences require an examination of the effect of leadership on teamwork and intergenerational conflict in the workplace.

Generation X employees are significantly higher in individualism than Baby Boomers. Generation X members would respond to working in teams as long as there is room for individual input rather than total team consensus.

The significant finding was that Baby Boomers are significantly more satisfied with their jobs and are less inclined to leave their position than Generation X employees. The authors attributed this to reduced coworker support found in Gen X employees. However, a noteworthy limitation of this study was that the sample came from one large organization.

Employers and researchers are becoming increasingly more interested in Millennials workforce characteristics as this generation has now become the largest in the United States. The following studies examine work-value differences between Millennials and the other generations in the workforce and support the arguments put forth by birth-year-cohort theorists.

Millennials as a cohort highly value learning, promotion, and a company's ethical standards as much as starting salary. Work values associated with Millennials employees include: (a) work should be done on my terms, with flexible work hours; (b) work is for earning money to purchase things; (c) work should be fun, friendly, and personal; (d) work should involve creativity, variety, innovation, and diversity; and (e) management opportunity should be immediate.

There are additional work-value differences between Millennials employees and the other generations in the workforce. Differences in Millennials compared to other generations that relate to the impact psychological traits can have upon the workplace. Millennials behaviors concern narcissism, which the authors suggest can destroy organizations. Managers who learn to understand these psychological differences will be more successful at supervising Millennials employees than those who ignore these disparities.

There also seems to be a significantly higher learning orientation in Generation X employees as compared to Baby Boomers. Generation X employees were found to have a strong desire for continuous learning and skills enhancement to be prepared for a sudden career change such as a lay-off. Getting ahead of this would suggest training for potential generational mentors and mentees should include interpersonal communication and good mentoring practices.

Leaders of a multigenerational workforce must learn to recognize the differences in characteristics of the various generations and develop a plan to use those differences to strengthen the organization through contributions by the workers. The attitudes, values, and beliefs of each generation affect how those workers view leadership.

Adapting a leadership style that is broad and flexible was more effective with a generationally diverse workforce. Managers who recognize each employee's generational perspective and allow an employee to perform duties more in accord with that perspective will see an increase in job satisfaction, organizational commitment, employee wellbeing, and productivity. Organizations should be aware of such generational work-value differences when it comes to management style as generationally diverse management personnel value different leader attributes.

Millennials managers should learn the values and characteristics associated with Baby Boomer employees. With the impending retirement of Baby Boomers, Millennials managers will probably manage Baby Boomer employees as they transition from the workforce. The younger-generation employee provided the older-generation employee with alternative ways to understand problems and develop new ideas.

Many organizations are now implementing a business strategy referred to as generational competence. Generational competence is the adoption of policies, benefits, and management styles by an organization to cultivate contributions from the most talented employees from all four generations. Programs that engage all generations in a mentoring program work best in spreading institutional knowledge, career progression, and visibility to all employees.

Millennials employees performed more effectively and made a larger impact on the organization's mission when provided with a nurturing, dynamic, and challenging workplace. This cohort values a workplace environment that includes state-of-the-art technology and flexibility as being more conducive to improved performance. The consequences of not providing such a context for the younger generation could cause conflict, poor performance, and costly turnover.

Many firms now spend more time with Millennials workers on employee progress and feedback. Millennials employees expected a clear direction and organization in the workplace. Millennials worker may be in favor of striving toward the corporate mission but may want to pick the tasks the employee undertakes and how those tasks are completed along the way. Baby Boomer managers and Millennials workers share more workplace commonalities than with Generation X managers.

75% of Millennials workers enjoyed working with Baby Boomers, and that nearly 60% turned to Baby Boomers for mentoring and advice rather than to Generation X managers. Millennials employees were loyal to organizations that provided professional development, mentoring, and advancement opportunities, and have a sense of corporate social responsibility.

Business leaders, who are capable of recognizing the generational work-value differences between workers, and applying leadership best practices to leverage the talents of their diverse workforce, can expect increases in organizational performance. Managers in today's U.S. workplace are supervising four generations of employees who researchers have found often experience high levels of intergenerational work-values conflict. Depending on the size and demographic composition of a manager's workforce, it may be necessary for managers to implement systems and procedures that are appropriately designed to meet the needs of four generations of employees and also align with the goals and objectives of the organization.

Establishing generationally appropriate clear communication between employees is an important aid in reducing generational conflict. To get this high standard, the leader must address and eventually implement open and frequent contact. Managers need to communicate the importance of technology to younger generations, the need to understand cross-generational cohort relationships, and the importance of passing tacit knowledge between generations.

Leadership was found to be a major factor in the successful operation of a multigenerational workforce. The leaders of a generationally diverse workforce who possessed the skills and abilities to comprehend the relevance and the importance of implementing communication and educational elements were more successful in reducing conflict among the generations. Managers who learned to recognize the differences in characteristics of the various generations developed a plan to use those differences to strengthen the organization through contributions by the workers.

Managers in the workplace need to supervise a multigenerational workforce most efficiently and effectively possible. Managers should understand work-value differences in employee behaviors and be able to make informed decisions about how they shape workforce strategies and management practices to get business results from a multigenerational workforce.

***

A direct relation to the idea of having the right talent is: how to properly conduct onboarding? Many people think onboarding is the same as new hire orientation. But I would say that's just how people work their way physically around the organization. How to speak the language of the organization, who the major players are, find the cafeteria, find the restrooms, etc. Onboarding is something different. It's all about making the employee feel welcome, and the time it takes for them to become proficient in their new job. That can be anywhere from six months to a year. Just because the job has been filled, just because we've hired someone in, doesn't mean that they're ready to go to work and return the investment of their hire. It just means they're in a position to learn the culture and become part of the organization. You can't go into a classroom for a day and know how to work and survive in the organization.

How do we make sure the employee is really welcomed during that time, so they feel that they're in a good place and have that happiness drive them to contribute their best? Additional responsibility is there for the hiring manager, how do they continue to make sure that top talent brought in can come into this critical role to help drive the business strategy and not leave?

Around the six-month mark is when the real employee shows up. It's when the person you hired is now in a position to show themselves for who they are. Right around this time is when the welcome can be challenging. You have hired this employee and are expecting great things from them, and if you do not see what you expect in those first few months, the welcome can become chilly. Things can change quickly for the employee. They might wonder whether or not they have really joined an organization that is exciting to them. The honeymoon is over at that point, as someone has said to me. At that six-month mark, is the match still made in heaven? Is there still a welcome feeling?

***

Some questions that help organizations get their mind around helping their leaders think differently.

- How generationally diverse is our workforce?
- What percentage will be retirement eligible within the next five years?
- Do we have the right competencies developed for leadership in strategic roles?
- Can we skill our talent up regardless of generation?
- What's the optimum balance of external hires and building talent within?
- What does that message send to our organization?
- Are we only pulling leaders from Baby Boomers or are we looking for knowledge, skill, and ability regardless of generation that allows them to be seen as leaders of the future?

When we think about bringing talent in and being proactive and planning for talent that we need.

- What's our average time to hire people in?
- Are we attracting generationally diverse talent and if not, why not?
- Do we have employee referral within the organization?
- How long does it take these employees across the generations to get them to a place of proficiency?
- Does it vary by generation?
- Does it vary by the hiring manager?
- By different parts of the organization?

- Where are we looking for talent?
- Are we using the best technology to find talent, or are we using antiquated ways?
- Does that limit us to a specific generation?

These are the types of things we want to think about. We want to bring in all types of talent. What do people think or feel or say when you tell them that you work for a particular company? Do people smile and nod or do they wince? Those things have value across generations. Traditionalists and Baby Boomers wanted to work for a big-name company that has the right name, right sound, which will be around for a while. That still exists to some degree in Gen X, but the opinion of colleagues is more important for Gen X and Millennials. Not just enough to have a big name, but it has to be the name of an organization known for treating its employees right.

HIRE FOR THE BEST FIT, NOT THE BEST RESUME

Recruiters are the ones out there on the front lines, trying to bring talent into organizations. Finding the right talent is where the true challenge lies. Will this person fit our organization? There are many meanings to that. Does the person look and feel to others like they belong here?

The answers to those questions play a huge role in successful talent acquisition. Unfortunately, recruiting and staffing are seen by the organization as an easy thing, as a lower level skill. On the contrary, finding the right talent for the organization is probably one of the hardest things to do.

Organizations sometimes shy away from being definitive about the type of person they want because they don't want to be viewed as being biased. I think this is erring too far on the side of political correctness. As a culture and a society, we've carried it way too far.

One of the biggest things that frustrate hiring managers is that recruiters take too long to get the talent the company needs. In reality, the business doesn't understand what the recruiter is doing.

When the hiring manager says, "I need a business development manager. I want them to have 10 years' worth of experience. I want them to have worked for a Fortune 100 Company, and have a wealth of potential client relationships. And, I want this person to live in the local area because I'm not paying for relocation."

All of these unique factors not only shrink the candidate pool and restrict the options of what the recruiter has to work with, but also increases time to hire. The recruiter takes this information and has to create the job requirement if it doesn't exist. That might take two or three days to write it, review it, post it, and start to field resume submissions from applicants. It might be three weeks or a month before the recruiter even starts to get candidates in for interviews from when the posting went up.

The hiring leader is then pissed off. "It's been two months. Where is this person I need?" Without constant contact from the recruiter back to the hiring leader, the hiring manager doesn't know the particulars of the situation, or what goes on behind the curtain. They think, "Next time I'll hire an outside agency so I can get this done in less time!"

Unfortunately, that's what happens to internal recruiters. They're out there with a flashlight in the middle of the daytime trying to find someone's shadow. They've been given this exacting description of what skills they need to find, but they haven't had the time to get a head start on trying to find that person. Then they get very little respect or thanks when they do find the needles in the haystack.

I think we're coming to a point where things are going to stabilize because nothing lasts forever—even the downturns, even the bad times. We're going to reach a point of stability. And when that does happen, you'll find a lot of organizations thinking, "We never want to go through that talent firefight again. We want to at least be able to mitigate our exposure to the whims and vagaries of the markets and economics." The only way to do that is to have as lean and as flexible an organization as possible. To do more with less, you have to have top talent.

You can't do more with less if the people that you've got can't pull it off. The best way to find those people is to grow them. You can't just hire them; because if you always hire from outside, it means that you had to go out and poach them, which costs money and isn't a long-term solution to a recurring problem.

Corporations and organizations over the past twenty years have had to resign themselves to hire and replace, hire and replace. If you don't have the type of talent management savvy that gives Gen Xers comfort enough about their career with your organization, they will go elsewhere, and you'll consistently need to hire and replace key employees.

There are serious questions that companies and organizations must now ask themselves:

- Do we want to continue to muddle along with this talent management thing and have things remain the same?
- Do we want the Board of Directors to continue to kick us to get a plan in place?
- Do we want to put the company into the position where the next time that there's an economic downturn or the competition has a decided advantage, and we're losing market share, we can compete?
- Do we want to invest in 'talent farming' now so that we can have the best talent in house to deal with whatever organizational challenges come next?

Don't continue down the path of trying to figure out what accommodates your need to feel comfortable, but is in opposition to getting results. Sometimes you have to get uncomfortable to get the result you want. You have to go through a period where it's going to be downright ugly as you shake things up, break things down, and build them back up stronger. A sustainable, proactive approach to talent management is the organization's displayed willingness to make a lasting cultural change.

Being stuck in the middle between having employees who can just barely do the job and in a place where they can do the job well is somewhere many organizations often find themselves. However, many are learning to recognize the warning signs, and know now how important it is to get it right when hiring for the best fit.

ORGANIZATIONAL CULTURE AS A PLAY IN THREE ACTS

We've talked about organizational culture, but haven't necessarily defined it for you. Part of that is because every culture is built on different values and beliefs. However, it's still useful to talk about the purpose of culture. In addition to it, helping cohorts define shared identities, beliefs, and practices, it also serves as a survival mechanism. Culture was created as a way for us to build patterns of interaction with one another.

Culture can really be defined in three segments. The most noticeable are the practices and artifacts that represent cultural norms. These are things such as dress and appearance, symbolism and stories/jokes. It's what most people and would immediately recognize, but culture goes deeper than that. The middle segment is represented by the values held within a group. These are represented by the aspirational value set, what we want to be, and the descriptive set, what describes good or bad in our culture.

Underlying all of this are a group's basic assumptions. It's the least questioned and the hardest to see for those within a group. It's thought patterns and perceptions, feelings and emotions, what's acceptable to show within your group and what's not acceptable. The basic assumptions tend to be brought to life when an outsider comes into the culture and begins to question things. This is fairly common when onboarding new hires or bringing consultants to an organization.

The challenge for organizations is to start thinking through the beliefs and values of their culture. When organizations begin this exercise, they can then start the process of aligning strategy, processes, and culture to truly start driving impact in their organization and industry.

People tend to revert to what's comfortable to them. It's in our nature to find the path of least resistance. Which means it's easier to call up and ask for favors from people you already know and people that you've been comfortable working with. This is where formal culture begins to break down. What arises is a black market, a place where favors are exchanged for silence and where people ask for compliance with the informal norms that are created and stood up.

For the employee, it becomes a balancing act of navigating the culture while also learning that patterns of interaction and actual work get done in a less formalized system. It becomes the 'dominant' culture for most individuals because their survival depends upon it. When work starts getting done through informal networks, it becomes a matter of compliance for many. It becomes easier to tell a white lie to the powers that be, with whom you interact with on an irregular basis, about how you accomplished a task than it does to directly confront or contradict those you work with day to day.

When this goes on long enough, strategies get questioned, processes start to fail, and people eventually ask why. This is usually when Stuck

On Start Coaching is brought in; at the moment when the leadership realizes that what they've done is try to push change onto their people without asking them for their support, their dedication or their commitment to the change. They may have explained the why and the how, but they failed to take into account the underlying cultural assumptions and norms that their culture supports. What they tried to change was the tip of the iceberg. If you truly want to see a change in an organization, start to focus on what's beneath the surface.

BUILDING CULTURE THROUGH SHARED EXPERIENCES

Organizational cultures are built over instances of time, but they can come crumbling down in a blink of an eye. You have to actively manage it. It's time you start paying heed to your organization's culture, both the formal and informal. You can talk to your employees about what works and what doesn't, and you can start making changes.

The quickest way to build a strong culture is through shared experiences. Nothing creates a bond like pulling together as a team on a project with a goal. It can be as simple as getting a project out the door under difficult situations, or it can be as fun as taking your teams out to participate in a day-long excursion. I've seen people take this to the extreme. It all depends on your risk threshold, but you can take your teams rock climbing, rafting, go-kart racing or just simply setting time to get out of the office and let loose.

Building culture is about building experiences that create trust and human connection. There's no one or easy way to get to this, but leaders should actively work to make it happen. Most organizations, especially large ones, don't provide the time and space for this to occur. They'd rather let the culture dictate to them than dictate the building of culture. It doesn't have to be this way. Look for opportunities to build experiences of human connection, and you'll see a difference in the way your teams respond and in the bond you're able to create.

A NEW OLD PREMISE: TREAT EMPLOYEES AS PEOPLE FIRST

Many of us have heard the age-old premise of "treat your employees as people first." It's a direct line to driving employee engagement, which helps curb issues with employee retention. So if we all know this, why is it also the premise that is often forgotten about?

I've got this novel approach for how to engage your people: try being more personable. Yes, it is as simple as that. It won't cost you anything but a little time, but it's time well spent. When you walk into work, try actually talking to your people. If it's been a while since you've done it, here's how it might look:

"Good Morning! How are you today?"

Do it while you're looking at them eye to eye. And then wait for a response. While you're waiting, try and listen to what they say. You can build tomorrows conversation off of what you heard today.

If your team is virtual, then start your conversation on the phone with, "Hello! How are you today?" and don't rush to fill in the silence.

Most of the time, people feel it's just a courtesy that's better to rush through and be done with, but it's about being real and drawing a connection with another person. As leaders, we set the tone for our people. If our people see us as too busy to engage or too frantic to take a moment with them, why should they be inspired by us? If you want to build a culture that your people can thrive in, it has to start with mastering the basics.

How often are you communicating with your team? How about with key stakeholders cross-functionally? Are there people in either of those groups that you're not talking with regularly? Do they know it? Are they aware that they're on the 'outside?' If you're unsure and can't answer these questions definitively, you should start tracking how often you interact with others and take note of the emotional climate as you interact with them.

Do this for a week or two and then lay it out graphically to see how often you're interacting with your team and key stakeholders. There's new research that shows effective teams are based on the patterns and frequency of communication between one another. Researchers at MIT have measured patterns and variables like tone, posture, and emotional resonance and have determined that this can help to make and keep teams highly effective.

There's another layer to this little experiment, and it's based on old research. Focusing on inclusion and exclusion into the 'in-group' should tune you into who's unable to contribute because their voice isn't being heard. Or conversely, you may find that they have the opportunity to contribute but are unwilling. Your question then becomes why. Is it because they lack the confidence to do so, or is it because they lack the ability?

This is a pretty simple experiment to run, but it will shed important light on how effectively your team is communicating and the patterns of your interaction with each of them.

As your culture matures, we can talk more about things like autonomy and purpose. But until then, keep it simple by starting with the easy stuff. You'll be amazed at the difference it makes. If you want to be the leader that positively impacts your people, engage them. Be nice, be human and be real.

IT'S NOT IN OUR CULTURE

Have you ever worked for an organization where it was proudly said, "We don't do it that way... it's not in our culture"? Well, I have, and I've worked with companies like this as an external consultant. It makes me wonder how receptive they are to change, and how easy it is to be innovative within the organization.

I'm not talking about cultural ethics at play in an organization, an aberrant behavior, or a devious decision. I'm talking about the way work gets done, the methods and procedures used to make something happen. Yes, I'm talking about playing within the rules, living up to ethical standards and doing things right. An example would be breaking up an organizational hierarchy, to remove a bottleneck to getting things done. Or it might be reaching across to a cross-functional partnership to move a process along. Work doesn't get done in a vacuum, but some organizations are structured like it does.

I've seen all too often when new people enter an organization or when a new organization is acquired. The unwritten social, cultural and political rules bear down on the newbie. They can be blindsided or derailed by it. Breaking the rules has consequences in these settings. The penalties for doing so outweigh the reward for taking a risk. Add to that the long memories of every miscue you have ever made, and you cannot recover.

We keep hearing about breakthrough thinking and innovation, but if your cultural rules, your rewards, and punishments, don't support taking risks or doing things differently, innovation will fall behind.

You acquire a company for a reason. You expect it to perform, to see cost efficiencies, you like their innovations, etc., so once you get things in order, don't squash what the company does best by being afraid of difference. It's okay to let them be different. Standardize platforms, integrate systems, move toward cost efficiency, but not disrupt the way work gets done. Similarly, you hire people for a reason. You expect them to perform, to get the job done, to innovate. So don't build cultural norms that get in their way.

If you want your people to thrive, especially the younger generations, give them the task and get out of the way. Be there to coach and to be an ear when needed, but don't smother them or hover over them. Just because it isn't done your way or the company way, doesn't mean that it will be done the wrong way.

MERGING TWO CULTURES INTO ONE

Like me, you may be surprised at the lack of work done on the people side of change when two organizational cultures merge. I'm not talking about the research, it's ample. So are the case studies in graduate school classrooms, the Time Warner/AOL merger comes instantly to mind as a classic example.

Despite all of the evidence, companies, and teams that are merging still focus on how the balance sheets line up and where the efficiencies lie than how the cultures align. But mergers and integration tend to fail because of the people practices. This is about more than just wholesale integration between two companies; this work should be done when integrating functions or teams. Due diligence should include how the people will integrate with one another, how the cultures line up and how to get the most out of your people. If you're thinking about merging teams or acquiring another organization, here are some things that you should be doing to make the transition smoother:

1. Create a change team that focuses solely on people
2. Examine performance policies and processes
3. Look at benefits and compensations
4. Understand what's on the table, what the tradeoffs are and what the implications for change are on the impacted parties
5. Give both sides a voice and a vote
6. Work directly with the business leads to align with their strategies

Most of what I have seen in my experience is that processes, technologies and the hard aspects of business are cared for up front. However, the people will be left to the last minute. Then the inevitable happens, we get the call from the leadership team asking why it isn't working. We get the call from the new organization struggling to achieve their business strategy during internal challenges. Why are people going to back channels? Why are they not just simply following the new protocols?

It isn't too late to fix when that call comes, but it's much more difficult, and it takes a lot longer. It's better to do the hard work of building a cultural integration strategy up front, rather than hope for a snappy HR "people policy fix" at the end of the deal. Give people the right amount of attention early on, and you'll see the difference pay off in the short-term. Plan for the culture change needed up front. It isn't only good for your business; it's also the right thing to do for your people.

ALIGNING CULTURES ACROSS GENERATIONS

One of the most difficult aspects of bringing two companies together is the integration of two cultures into one. We are not asking for both entities to lose a sense of self, but we are asking that they learn to assimilate new practices, new ideas, and new processes into a broader macro-culture.

I like to think about it as the European Union. If you think aligning the cultures of two organizations is tough, consider how difficult it must be for the French to integrate into a broader cultural exchange. Not to go into a political science lesson here, but the French are simultaneously trying to integrate immigrants into the French culture, maintain the cultural legacy of what it means to be French amid globalization, and adapt to the new social, cultural and political realities brought forth by the European Union. So if you're struggling through a cultural integration at your company, it could be a lot more challenging. There isn't a one-size fits all remedy for how to bring together two disparate organizational cultures.

There are a set of tools and practices, that when used correctly, will help you get through the integration. Most importantly, you need to start aligning the two cultures during the due diligence process. It's often overlooked, because the focus tends to be on the books, the numbers, and the efficiencies, but if you cannot get the people to buy in, then you have a much larger issue at hand. Running a diagnostic up front allows you to assess the cultural readiness of the organizations and will give insight into how the employees from both organizations feel about the merger.

This isn't to say that you use the assessment to prevent the merger from occurring, but it gives perspective into the areas that you'll want to address early on in the process. Forming a steering committee is a good way to start evaluating the two cultures and the practices that are up for debate.

Most organizations also bring in outside help because it provides a fresh set of eyes to point out cultural aspects that may go unnoticed by incumbents.

The Leverage Goes to the Talented

A few years ago, I had the opportunity to hear Dan Pink speak at an event. Something he said has been banging around in my mind for days: "Organizations need talent more than talent needs organizations." I looked at my colleague sitting beside me and had the light bulb flick on. It isn't necessarily a new way of thinking about talent, but it's a clean way. And if you're in the talent business at a large organization, it has to shake you to the core a bit. You don't have the leverage the way you used to have when you're trying to bring people into your organization or stopping them from leaving your organization. Your leverage is gone! Organizations gave up a good deal of their leverage when they opted for more flexibility. Roles were no longer safe from the chopping block. Employee loyalty was no longer rewarded or recognized. It was the business and the profit that mattered.

You know the story, roles off-shored and organizations went flat, fewer people, less overhead, more profits. But the tides are turning. Once the stability of organizational life went, so too did loyalty. You wanted flexibility? Well, you have it now. It's so flexible in fact that the company can do just fine without you. I guess that in the late 80s and 90s nobody could have predicted it to become this extreme. Organizations still have the capital, resources, and wherewithal to do great things, but technology has leveled the playing field.

If you're talented and you have an idea, you don't need direct organizational support to make it happen. You can go alone. And people enjoy it. I happen to be one of them. According to a report by MBO Partners, the rate of independent workers has gone up 5.5% in the last few years. No doubt some of that has to do with layoffs and restructuring, but don't expect independents to return to organizations when the economy turns. MBO also projects that by 2020 the independent workers will account for more than 50%. So, if you're in the talent management or talent acquisition business and you're making a case for why talent should consider coming to you, it better be a good one because you're swimming against the current.

BRANDING LEARNING AND DEVELOPMENT

What's the learning and development (L&D) brand at your place? Do you even have an L&D brand? Would your employees recognize any of your offerings? Do people want in, or are they forced to want in? For as long as I can remember, we haven't done much in the way of branding and marketing our internal programs. We've let them be, and it shows. I still see learning with clip art plastered all over it. It makes me laugh, and not the gut-roaring kind, but the sarcastic, "I cannot believe this is serious," kind.

Learning and development may be a drain on the corporate dollar, but if we are to believe that it's the people that make the difference in our organizations, then we need to put the money where our mouth is. Building development that people want to be a part of makes sense. Putting dollars behind that development also makes sense. So why is it that we still have courses that look like they were created at the dawn of the Internet age?

Why not brand our learning so that substance matches style? Do your people even know what you offer? Are they compelled to go to training because of the quality of the content or are they mandated to attend to meet some goal for the year? Could they tell you what it means to be in your high potential development programs? Do they understand the value that these programs create? If you cannot answer yes to these questions, then you need to consider what you're doing to brand and market your offerings. It's time that you get clear in the value that you bring and the purpose that you serve.

ANSWERING THE QUESTION OF FIT

There's a moment in the employee life cycle when they're forced to confront the inevitable question of fit. Are they a fit for the role? The more important question is, are they a fit for the organization? Technical skills can be taught (to an extent), and a coach or mentor can get you up to speed on how the organization operates and how the business runs. But the question of fit isn't one that anyone but you can answer.

Fit is all about social-awareness. You need to pick up the cues. You need to take the responsibility to understand how the organization runs, how people interact, how work gets done and how people become successful in their careers. Not everyone gets it. Do you want to conform to the organizational culture, or do you want to remain on the fringe? It's ultimately the employees' call, but it comes with consequences for all involved. The consequences can range from minor disassociation and feelings of exclusion to more serious concerns that may result in performance management.

So how do you combat the issue? What actions have you taken? Do you hire for fit? Are you looking for fit when you screen applicants? Are you asking the right, behaviorally based questions? Does your team know what a good fit looks like? If I were to ask you to describe what a good fit looks like, how similar will your responses be? Are they aligned? If not, it's time that you start talking about what good looks like on your team and in your organization. We're moving too quickly in today's world to let a poor fit drag down the productivity of the whole. It's never an easy thing to do, but it's in the best interest of all involved to cut your losses sooner rather than later. If you've made a mistake, and they don't fit, do everyone a favor and move the person along to where they can be successful.

CHANGE IS EVERYWHERE

It seems to me that change is at the very core of what we do in today's world. Whole industries have been re-imagined, innovations we couldn't see coming ten years ago are now mainstream fads. By now we understand the changes that took place in the mobile space, the music industry, medicine, and the defense industry.

Even education, typically the most resistant to change and latest to the party, has begun a transformation that many are still reluctant to accept. Massive, open, online courses (MOOCs) have started to emerge. They're flipping the model of education upside down and are providing access to millions of people worldwide to learn about topics that have been traditionally available only to students at some of the most prestigious institutions of learning.

We can assume that colleges will no longer be able to charge at a price point of $50,000 a year. It also brings to question the value of a four-year degree if you can develop competencies that are more tailored to specific roles and functions by enrolling in a class when and where you want. We can also imagine MOOCs having a longer-term impact on consulting and in particular leadership development because the research that drives much of this work is now free, readily available and taught by the professors who have done the work.

The model of content being king is quickly eroding. What we're learning is that now it's about application and building experiences to support the content. Change is here; it's everywhere, and now it's up to us to re-imagine our own industry. We can't sit idly by and wait for things to happen. HR hasn't traditionally been known for innovation, but neither has education. It's time we start doing things differently around here.

Setting Business Strategy as an Imperative

A.G. Lafley, former head of global consumer giant, P&G, put forth a five-step template on how to think about strategy in your organization. It's a solid foundation to start from because it gets at the heart of what strategy is all about. Identifying opportunities, understanding the tradeoffs and ultimately making choices.

Here are the five questions that he frames up as critical when thinking about strategy:

1. What's your winning aspiration?
2. Where will you play?
3. How will you win?
4. Which capabilities must be in place?
5. What management systems are required?

What is important to note is that these questions transcend industries, organizations, functional groups, and roles. You can apply them anywhere to help you think about your go forward strategy. They're extremely helpful as a baseline when you're considering a new acquisition. If done correctly, the answers to these questions help you set the context for the "What" and the "How" and help you to look for alignment between your organizational mission and your strategic intent.

During your planning, don't be too eager to jump past question number one. Your decision to go forward should be based on how closely you align to the corporate mission and whether or not this move would pull you too far away from that mission.

Setting strategy is a go slow to move faster proposition. To do it right, you need to bring the right level of analysis to each of the five questions, and you need to be prepared to alter course along the way. Don't be afraid of new insights but don't ever lose sight of your corporate mission.

CHAPTER 2

How to Help Employees Feel Valued

Engagement isn't just about employees being happy. Engagement is what we do and say to make them feel valued. When we hire professionals, we want them to demonstrate their expertise and bring innovation and creative thoughts while looking at our organization through new eyes. Do we have a culture that rewards innovation, different thinking? Is it excited about ways people of different generations, ethnicities, genders, see business challenges and opportunities?

Engagement isn't pizza parties and ice cream. It's far from that. It's a workforce that comes to work and fills the whole time they're there and feel valued for what they bring to the table. Where they can go home at the end of the day feeling like they work for an organization that wants them there, needs them there, and is going to become better because they're there.

**

When we think about employee development, it's not just sending people to training. It's much more than that. When we think about training adding value, training should inform what you're doing next. I see leaders sending employees to training to get fixed. Development means giving people opportunities. Stretch assignments, doing next level work, and working in areas they might be interested in growing. All those things add value.

Many times, I talk to senior leaders within organizations only to hear them say that they "Don't know what these kids want." Ask them. Each employee is different. Each has specific needs and desires for how they want to participate in the workforce. We're trying to set up an environment inside organizations where leaders have the opportunity to talk to their employees about what they want and need. More importantly, employees are working in organizations where they feel they can have a conversation with their leaders about different opportunities.

Without those levels of trust, without having the types of leaders willing to engage with that conversation, it challenges us from having the workforce that values the difference across generations. We get so wrapped up into how the work needs to get done, we forget about what the work actually is.

That's when I see the biggest differences across generations. It's not the fact that one wants to work less than another, but how the work is done. Baby Boomers, Gen Xers, Millennials, and Gen Z can each achieve the same outstanding results with a task, but how they go about it will look and sound drastically different. They might work different hours or use different technology. That doesn't mean one is more committed than the other.

***

One of the things I had great success with as a hiring manager is that I always gave my employees a look at what was needed, why it was needed, when it was needed, and sometimes where it was needed. I never told them how to go about doing their work. I felt if I was hiring in the best of the best, I shouldn't need to tell them how to do their job. Quite frankly, it would be insulting.

Many of the folks entering the workforce from Gen Z will want to work in a way that adds value. They don't want to be an automaton. They don't want to be told what to do, relegated to the sidelines, or told "my way or the highway."

I talk to my students who are Gen Z often, and I look at engagement surveys. There is a stark reality that has emerged. My research tells me that Millennial and Gen Z employees don't feel like they have the opportunity to really contribute in a way they want to. They feel they need to wait their turn or ask for permission or they have a manager who is more worried about the way the work gets done rather than the fact that the work gets done at all. It's very important to allow folks to have what they want and be seen as someone who really is valued for their expertise. Valued for how they have spent their time getting to that place in the organization. Valued because they're doing it a different way than before because it's needed.

Many organizations have these outstanding learning and development department, but I often look at those departments and wonder what it is they're doing. Are they developing people for the knowledge, skills, and ability they need just for today? Or have they done strategic workforce planning to take a look at what they'll need in the future? A look at the workforce today shows there's a gap in what we have and what we need so let's develop the skills and knowledge to close that gap.

We already know the answer to that. Many learning and development departments are in place to teach very generic, basic things. I've worked in a corporate university, and I've worked where there's been a learning and development arm of the business. The folks that do the real development work are not the folks at the corporate university. No disrespect to my colleagues who work in a corporate university structure and think it's the greatest thing since sliced bread, but I have been in different business units where the leaders are challenged up the minute, to close development gaps in their employee base. We need a course in doing business in Brazil, can you help us? And they go to the corporate university and are told sorry, we only do enterprise-wide needs, like project management or communications training or leadership development.

That's great, and all, but the business needs something different. What do those in the corporate university or L&D often say? "Well, it's the business' responsibility for functional skills training. We don't do that." Well, guess what? The majority of the training that your workforce needs is functional skills. Sure it's great to have leadership programs. I've made my bread and butter around leadership programs. But the business is charged with executing a strategy to make money. The business is the owner of the two key performance indicators (KPIs) of any organization... making the company money and or saving the company money. HR and talent management is the arm of the organization with the charge to support these initiatives.

If they aren't doing our jobs to give the business what they need, when they say they need it, then they're not doing our job. Business leaders need trusted advisors and partners. A business partner would help the business by being right there with them, understanding their strategy.

For me, I think that having development tied to immediate need is important. When I look at organizations that I have the opportunity to work with which might be struggling with expansive growth over the next five years, they're not turning to their HR counterpoints, or corporate university with their large catalog of e-learning courses and outsourced vendor delivered courses where people come in and spend a day in training. They're looking at external consultants to close the gap between knowledge, skill, and ability now and knowledge, skill, and ability needed going forward. There's a succinct challenge here to do that.

So how do you mind that gap between the generations? Every single person in your organization, regardless of generation, want to do their best. They realize to feel valued; they have to deliver value. No greater way to make an employee feel valued than investing in them by helping them bridge the gap between the knowledge they need versus the knowledge they have. That's not always training. It could be a cross-functional assignment; it could be the opportunity to work on a project team. There are a lot of different ways we can make the employees in our organization feel valued.

***

Are our leaders really measuring engagement, and if so, how often are they doing it? If you were to talk to your leaders, talk to your HR department, your talent managers, do they have an overall sense of the level of engagement in the organization? Do they know where how people are feeling about working there? And if they do know, what are the engagement levels of the top talent employees in strategic roles? Do they know the level of engagement regardless of the generation of employees who are within their first 18 to 36 months of employment within the organization? Are the hiring managers in a place where they're having engagement conversations regularly or is it just talked about at the end of the year? Are we actually having conversations, and if we are, have those managers been really training to improve employee engagement or are they just placating the employee? Is there commitment to making things better or is it just sitting around thinking about what will happen next?

What's happening there? Are our leaders within the organization thinking about how engagement is related to productivity, and if there's a lack of engagement, how that really does signify the fact that the turnover is there? How does it point to an engagement problem? If they're engaged, they're not going to leave, and if they don't leave, there won't be retention issues.

While they're there, how do you develop them? How do you keep them from being marginalized and undervalued? If they're at 75% with their knowledge, skill, and ability, what are you doing to get them that other 25%?

So, you might ask your leaders:

- Are the develop programs more than just sending people to training?
- Are learning and development really developing knowledge and skills or is it just learning for learning's sake?
- Do managers understand the strengths, interests, and aspirations of their employees?
- Can employees talk to their leader or are they just going to training to keep their manager quiet?
- Are action learning projects embedded into the training programs or is it just go to training for a day, get a big binder and good luck to you?
- Do you get a chance to practice what you learned? Or are you just expected by osmosis to have the way you're going to do your job change?
- Is social media employed in communication and learning programs? Do you use social media at all? Do we realize that the generations have different feelings and places in their lives for social media?
- Do employees have options and choices in achieving their development goals, and if not, then why not? Why don't they have those options? Why can't there be a conversation with the leader, why isn't there a conversation available in the culture that allows them to talk about what they would like to do?

Finally, one big thing comes to mind about organizations that are successful in minding that gap. They have an eye on which leaders have the reputation of being talent builders. Those are the types of people that Millennials, and Gen Z employees will seek out. Those who are knowledge sharers, not knowledge hoarders. We want to work for leaders that will develop and build us, not just bring us in and tell us to wait until we've been here "long enough." Are you creating the kind of environment where younger talent coming are made to feel like they're sitting at the kid's table?

What drives value, and allows employees to feel value is the responsibility of the leader to get to the place where they can understand the employee and have a relationship with the employee. When trust is there, engagement and development don't just become words but become part of the culture of the organization. If you have that, then you're well on your way to minding that gap between generations.

TAPPING INTO THE POWER MOTIVE

One way to build engagement in employees is to tap into their power motive. Find out what drives them and where they want to make an impact. You need to find the time during your day to let your employees know that they're still relevant. The power motive is about the impact that your employees think they can have based on the role and the assignment given to them. It's about what they can control and sometimes whom they can control.

In his research, the late David C. McClelland made a case for two types of power motives. One is personal, and the other is institutional. As a leader, your goal is to get your employees to buy into the institutional power motive. The difference in the two lies in the way the power is manifested and the way it shows up in the environment. The personal power motive is about acquiring the power to direct others. The institutional aspect of power is about influencing others to achieve the goals of the organization. If you can tap into the institutional aspect of the power motive to get your people inspired, you can increase engagement, empowerment and bottom-line results.

The big question is how do you do it? It starts with being attuned to your people and the culture of your organization. It isn't rocket science, but I don't want to minimize the work or the importance of doing it. It's really about taking the time to coach your people, to listen to them and see what motivates their behaviors. It may be about seeking power and making an impact, or it may be about staying on course and not taking risks because they don't want to fail.

The Classic Burning Platform

Organizations that effectively engage employees have a significant advantage over competitors. Disengaged workers are actively seeking new opportunities as the economy grows, while competitors are looking for ways to gain an edge by actively pursuing your high performers. Growth remains a top strategic priority for nearly half of all organizations, while many organizations continue to focus on profitability. Innovation, efficiency and high-quality performance will be key to success, but a lack of engagement and loss of talent will seriously impact your organization's ability to meet strategic objectives.

Organizations need strong performers, working smarter and more productively, with competent leaders who will engage and motivate them to meet growth goals. Are you at risk of losing top talent? Are your employees engaged in their work and with the organization? New research has given us a clearer insight into key issues that impact an employee's decision to leave his or her current employer. Not surprisingly, the top five drivers cited by employees as most important to engagement include base pay, stress levels, promotion opportunity, work/life balance and confidence in senior leadership.

Losing key players means spending money to recruit, train, and get new employees up and running as contributors. It could also mean declines in productivity, lost business opportunities and weakened customer relationships. Employee turnover impacts other employees as well, contributing to increased workloads and stress, further eroding engagement and creating an environment of discontent.

Performance Reviews = Futility

Annual performance reviews are losing popularity because leaders realize that is practice is antiquated at best. I would estimate that 75% of companies still force them onto employees and teach their managers to be talking heads, ready to critique every move you make. For most of my career in corporate America, these conversations have been a joke. I do believe strongly in the talent review process, but I think it should be more transparent.

The core of any successful review rests in the foundational processes used to bring leaders up to speed on what's expected, the language that needs to be used, the definitions used for high potential, how the organization defines a person as ready now for more responsibility, and the commitment to action an organization is willing to make. Action coming out of the review is critical. It's great to identify and discuss who the top talent is in any organization, but taking action to prepare them for broader and more complex roles is where the rubber meets the road.

I've sat in on numerous performance review discussions where potential steps to improvement are laid out for a faltering employee but have also then 12 months later witnessed how nothing has happened. The manager didn't have a meaningful discussion with the employee about their performance. Or, they had a single conversation and expected the change to just happen without following up. This then leaves the employee unaware of where they fit. Worse, the employee has not been told of the potential the organization sees in them.

I've seen this scathing lack of action and commitment come back to bite the organization. The star employee doesn't know where she stands. She loves the organization and her work, but she's not willing to wait around to be told of her worth. Because her leader is not showing her any commitment to her development, she decides to jump. What I've found in most organizations is a lack of consensus on what, when, and how to talk to your employees, so managers tend to shy away, not knowing what they can or can't share. It's this lack of clarity that creates confusion and mismanagement.

THE MISCONCEPTIONS OF ENGAGEMENT

There's a line of thought out there that if you want happy employees, all you need to do is pay them well and give them a little positive reinforcement. The only problem with this thinking: it's just not true. If you want to raise the performance bar in your world, you need to actually engage your employees. Try connecting with your employees as people first and employees second.

In fact, the consulting firm, Aubrey Daniels International tells us it's as quick as a three-minute meeting. That's it. It doesn't take much. It just takes some thought and some effort. Positive reinforcement is about making your employees feel empowered. It's about asking them how they successfully navigated a project. It's sharing that information with others, and it's about being consistent in your actions.

The beauty of the three-minute meetings is that it happens every day. If done correctly, you won't have to hold hour-long sessions waiting for your employee to unload on you. In this meeting, you can gain insight into what's working and what's not, and you can help employees self-correct. You have an opportunity to provide them with immediate and certain reinforcement. This is about providing immediate interpersonal satisfaction. You teach them to see what's working and why. If done well, you suddenly have people raising the bar on their own.

We rush from meeting to meeting. We go frantically running through the office, only to approach someone with a need or a reprimand. If you don't think that's you, watch and see how your employees or colleagues react when you step out of your office door. Are they head down and avoiding eye contact? If so, you have some work to do. If you're only engaging your employees when something has gone wrong, or want something from them, then you need to find a new style. If your only form of positive reinforcement is offering congrats and a bonus at the end of the year, you really need to rethink your approach.

EVOLUTION AS CULTURAL CHANGE

Most organizations that I've consulted with or have worked for primarily focus their talent management efforts on a small cadre of individuals. These folks are commonly known as "high potentials" within the organization. The field of leadership development and talent management has been explicit in its focus of narrowing efforts toward the few and the mighty.

It makes sense in a world of limited resources, reach and scope, but things are changing. Technology and new techniques have disrupted the standard norms and allowed us to expand our focus and attention to meet the needs of the masses. Only we haven't done so yet. Not most of us anyway. Instead, we continue the traditional paradigm of learning, development, and selection. We keep moving forward with deference to the norms and values of the past, we've been reluctant to rock the boat and to try new, innovative strategies for growing our people.

The fact remains that a high tide raises all boats and the tide for many organizations is finally coming in. Imagine a world where we don't let good performers slip through the cracks, a world where we focus on raising everyone, where good performance becomes great. Imagine a workplace that's engaged and committed to getting things done because they know that the organization shows them the same commitment. The option is available to us. We can start thinking more broadly about how to develop people and build better workforces.

Technology gives us a scale that we've never had before. New management theories and a better understanding of how people work enable us to offer smarter and timelier opportunities to our employees. These opportunities should be about both targeting individual needs and opportunities that offer scale across the breadth of your organization. Focusing our efforts on a narrow few doesn't raise the tide for the entire organization; it ignores the masses, the core of your labor force, and relies too heavily on a trickle-down approach to management. We need to start thinking more holistically about developing our people, the workforce is changing, and we should too.

CHAPTER 3

HOW TO HELP YOUR EMPLOYEES BE THEIR AUTHENTIC SELF

Being my authentic self is very important to me. And I think is it to most people, but those same people allow themselves to ignore that importance for compensation. Many times, you go through the interview process, the courtship, and the organization thinks they know who they're getting and the employee thinks they know who they're joining, and six months in both realize it's a wrong fit. It can come out in many different ways: lack of engagement, voluntary separation from the organization, people being let go.

When you go through the process of finding a talented individual and then at six months in they aren't returning the investment, that's almost the same as leaving.

When a person comes to work, can they be who they are or do they have to put on a mask to be part of your culture? When we go through the interview process, we're all on our best behavior. What's interesting is that those who make the right match are not on their "best" behavior; they're on their real behavior.

Across the generations, talking about what the employee needs is paramount. We can use blanket statements for what Millennials want or what Gen Xers want, but every employee is different. They all need different things. We need to think about holding onto the talent we need and let them be their authentic selves, even more so with Gen X and Millennial generations. Not being able to be yourself or work the way you want to work challenges the employees from being able to be themselves. If you have to leave half, or really any of yourself, in the car or on the train just so you can stay employed, that will wear on you. Not being your authentic self shows up in the form of stress. In my opinion, stress is what we feel when we spend time doing something we don't want to do, trying to be someone that we don't want to be, or trying to control something that is out of our control.

We've created a system where work is the dominant activity of our lives from the ages of 22 to 67. Given that we spend the majority of our waking hours working, shouldn't we identify with our work? Shouldn't we look for meaning in our day to day? I understand that certain situations require people to make things happen, regardless of purpose or meaning in their day to day, but for those of you who found work that you tolerate or even enjoy, it's time that you look for purpose in your work.

I'm defining purpose as more than maximizing shareholder returns or lining your own pockets. We all have our basic needs, and for many of us that includes doing well by our family and being able to provide them a comfortable life, but when thinking about your own purpose in what you do, don't simply stop there. There's more underlying that, it may be self-empowerment, it may be about helping others, it may be about fulfilling a desire to learn and to be intellectually challenged, or it may be about introducing new ideas into the workplace.

Tap into it. It's good to let it surface. It can be very personal, and it can be individualistic, it doesn't always have to be about the greater good for everyone, and that's okay. If you can identify your purpose, it's an extremely powerful force for self-development. It brings new meaning to what you do, you will start to look at things differently, and you will look for ways to maximize your impact by keeping your purpose top of mind.

Another way to conceive of this exercise is to think about legacy. What's the legacy that you want to leave behind? How do you want to be known and remembered by others? Make the sub-conscious become conscious. If you can identify the *why*, you'll feel good about the *how*.

I say to some of my consulting clients that you can retain top talent by appealing to three focus areas. Heart, head, and wallet.

1. Head: Are you appealing to the employees thinking that this is the right thing for their career? What they're doing for the skills they have, are they mentally stimulated, are they able to participate, are they able to wrap their minds around ways to add value.
2. Heart: Something we see now more than ever in Gen Xers, Millennials, and especially Generation Z. Am I working for an organization that I believe in? Does it make my heart feel good to work here? Do I agree with the mission and leadership? Do they even look believable? Can I get up every day and feel good about going to work?
3. Wallet: Often thought of the number one reason people stay at an organization, which isn't true. Do you pay someone what they're worth? Do you pay them fairly for their contributions?

Do they feel their salary is fair considering how they feel in their heart and the thoughts in their head?

These three focus areas are in connection, and in harmony are what make it all work. Everyone in the workforce, regardless of generation, is looking for a job that allows them to be their authentic self while having their heart, head, and wallet are being appealed to.

Many of us go to work at a job that gives us two of the three. I don't know of anyone, myself included, that might stay at an organization where you only get one. Even money. You could be very well paid but be in a toxic environment, or not agree with leadership, or perhaps they are not welcoming, or you may have witnessed something being done that was unethical.

As a leader, you have to know your employees as people first. What they want, what they're about. What we can do as an organization to create an environment where retention becomes the norm. Why did this person join the organization? If this person is a top talent, why did they join? What keeps them there? Trying to find out these things are important because then if you know what keeps someone there and excited, you know what you can emphasize. The most important question is what would cause them to leave. If you know what would cause them to leave, and find out that's tied to them having to be someone they're not, that speaks volumes. You might find out that what will allow them to be their authentic self is for them to move to another place in the organization.

These are the types of real conversations that leaders need to be willing to have with their employees. There are going to be times where they aren't the right fit, but let it be that decision after having done everything possible after hiring the employee. Don't just say it didn't work and push them out the door. Even if you think it will save heartache down the line, it still causes destruction to your organization. People are watching. Those that are left behind, those that might have been hired in at the same time, they're watching and learning what it means to be in the organization.

***

As leaders, we should indeed start to think from a talent management perspective about generation dynamics and the gaps that can emerge when you do not seek to bring the best out of your people. Here are some questions to help you have a direct conversation with your HR business partners:

- What's the turnover in different generations?
- What's the turnover for hard to fill jobs overall?
- Do they come in and then leave in three years?
- Do we see a great amount of turnover in the Millennial population?
- Are there leaders being held accountable for losing valuable employees? If they aren't, why not?
- Are we looking at the organization, thinking about the strategy?
- If we're in place to get results, and the only reason we're here is to make money or save money, what are we doing to ensure we have the workforce in place to do that?
- This multigenerational workforce is made up of different wants and needs and desires, so what are we doing to ensure we're meeting those expectations?

Answering these questions can help to drive retention. Are we not only building for right now but also for the future? It does us little good to build for tomorrow when we haven't figured out how to keep employees today. That authentic self means a lot. We spend a lot of time at work, and all of us want to belong to an organization where we feel that our best interests and best gifts are on display and utilized.

WHEN THE WORK GOES UNNOTICED

There are days that you sit in your office and hide from work. You put it off and wait another day. Every little thing easily distracts you. You check the weather. You check the news. You grab a coffee. You hide. You go unnoticed in plain sight.

Then there are the days that you're so consumed by your work that you forget to grab lunch. Your conversations are short, hurried and brief. You don't even have time to check social media on your smartphone! You in a perpetual rush, you're frantic, but you're delivering. The only problem is, no one notices. You're still hidden in plain sight. People see you in distress, and each interaction that you had was so frantic, you have pushed people away. Maybe they're talking, and if so, it isn't in a good way.

If this sounds like you, ask yourself: how do people know about the work you do? I know in most organizations they measure success based on metrics and results, but what are you doing to show your true value to the organization if what you do goes unnoticed? Sometimes the harder you work, the deeper you dig and the more invisible you come. I'm not suggesting that you stop working and loaf about. You need to find a balance. You need to own what you do well and make sure people know it. Be confident, not arrogant.

If you want to move in your career, think about who sees you, what they see, and go do something about it. Take the time to walk the floors. Check in frequently with your people. Learn to lead and guide others.

Build Your Informal Network

An article by John Kotter in the November 2012 issue of Harvard Business Review got me thinking deeply about the duality of organizations. In every organization, there is the formal and the informal network. And within each of those, there are nexuses of power dynamics that arise. In the traditional and more formal organizational structure, you have command and control. People gain power based on title and place. In the informal organizational structure, the network, people gain power through information and connections.

Kotter names this distinction, and challenges companies to accept the distinction and to embrace it. The article talks about creating a dual structure where the network is uninhibited by bureaucracy structures. The challenge for most companies is that people are resistant to change, and creating an informal network that focuses on strategy and isn't controlled by a formal hierarchy is ripe for resistance.

The irony is that it's already in place... you just haven't named it. And more importantly, you haven't sanctioned it. It operates like a favela in Rio de Janeiro. You know it's there, it's impossible to miss, but because the law hasn't sanctioned them, they operate under a veil of secrecy. But they're organized. They have structures and rules; they have guiding coalitions that are responsible for the upkeep and in that way they gain legitimacy.

So the question is: what's taking you so long? Why not name it, sanctioned it and use the informal network to inspire and engage your people? Maybe you just haven't paid much attention to its existence.

Maybe you know it's there, but you refuse to believe in its inherent value. Whatever the case, it's time you embraced it.

If you're unsure of what it looks like, ask people in your organization how they get work done. Do they go through the formal hierarchy, or do they work around people? My bet is they move around the hierarchy to get work done.

Engagement Levels As Cause for Concern?

Employee engagement really hasn't rebounded to post 2008 levels yet, but we continue to ask employees to do more with less. If we can solve for engagement issues, the gains reaped in productivity and the savings from retaining employees would be material. Engagement levels have tanked since the Great Recession, for many reasons. The culprits that we've identified are obvious, but impactful. Budget cuts, stagnant wages, lack of advancement and mobility opportunities, and most importantly... the lack of empowerment and autonomy given to employees.

Employee groups lost the autonomy and the control to do their work effectively. Leaders in this economy were more prone to trust seasoned veterans to turn the ship around than new employees with innovative ideas. This has profound impacts on how engaged our employees are and how we're managing opportunities for them to grow and develop.

During the Great Recession, it was easy for leaders to cut budget dollars attributed to talent development, but it was also short-sighted. It's created a backlog in the talent pipelines of organizations. Younger, up and coming, talent hasn't seen the movement or the development that they were looking for, and as a result, we've seen engagement levels correspondingly drop.

To revive lagging engagement levels, disengage your leaders. Ask them to start focusing on talent while keeping an eye on the business, but allowing their people to do the work. If you want to engage your employees, allow them to make an impact. It's what they've been waiting for. Give them the insights and the tools to do their jobs, coach them to excellence in execution, and step out of the way of their innovation.

THE INVALUABLE CULTURE OF TRUST

Research on building trust in organizations was released by Interaction Associates and the Human Capital Institute. They look at how high performing organizations build trust through three key behaviors. It's important because they note that trust is built, not inherently present like most organizations and leaders believe. Trusting that you'll pay me at the end of the week isn't what we're talking about here.

Trust is defined by the authors as: 'The willingness to put oneself at risk based on another's actions.' It's a simple, yet elegant definition of trust and it's an important question to ask of your employees and your leaders. Are they willing to put themselves at risk for your actions? It's the fundamental keystone in building a high performing culture because everything grows from here. Culture thrives on trust. If you want engaged employees, they need to trust you. If you want to build that trust, you need to be out front leading the charge. You need to be the role model. It starts at the top.

The research confirms this. They call it "predictable transparency." People like consistency. They want to be led by leaders who are consistent in their actions, have clearly defined values, and are transparent in the way they operate. It's not rocket science, but it's not easy. If it were easy, there wouldn't be an entire multi-million-dollar industry helping organizations and leaders trying to make it right. And quite frankly, Stuck On Start as a boutique consulting firm focused on equipping leaders to manage and lead the current workforce would not have any clients.

We talk a lot about culture at Stuck On Start Coaching because we know that fundamentally it's what makes organizations tick. We know it's not easy to pay attention to the 'touchy, feely,' side of the organization structure. Most leaders are uncomfortable in this space because they don't see the evidence right away. Intuitively, we all know it impacts the bottom-line. The smart money is on leaders working to create a culture of trust if they want the organization to perform well and win in the marketplace.

THE EMPLOYEE FEEDBACK LOOP

Culture may be set from the top, but it's lived from the bottom up. It's the experience of the employees' day in and day out that creates how the culture lives, thrives or dies in an organization. We've talked in the past about the formal and the informal distinction of any organizational culture. The formal is what's espoused and talked about; the informal is what's lived reality for most employees in the organization. It's this reality that you should be focusing on when you implement a change because it's in the informal culture where the truth about the policies is spoken, and it's here where ideas to help implement the change are discussed. It's up to you to fish them out.

In a former organization, I used to hear a senior executive tell every leader in the organization that it was their job to talk to a customer and a customer-facing employee every day. The rationale was that you couldn't get the reality of what was happening in your organization by simply talking to your direct reports. They had too much at stake to let it all out. But the customer and the frontline employee would tell you the truth even if it was painful.

What mechanisms do you have in play at your organization to feed information up to leadership? If you don't have something in place, you need to, and it's a simple fix. You can start by talking to your frontline employees. You can implement a share point for them to provide open and direct feedback. You can create a drop box for the employees to pitch ideas. But, if you do any of these things, you need to act on them. You can't just let them sit and not take any action. You also cannot *not* communicate the results of the actions taken.

It gets challenging when you try and make the change in your leadership. You need your leaders to ask the right questions. You need them to learn how to handle tough feedback. You need them to create an environment where it's understood that providing feedback isn't just ok, but it's expected. To do this, you need to set the tone at the top. You need to reflect these behaviors day in and day out.

My suggestion: reward those who speak up and speak out for the good of the organization.

INSTALLING A CULTURE OF TRANSPARENCY

Building nimble and agile organizations requires a level of transparency that most organizations are currently ill-prepared to undertake. The steps to get there are simple on paper, but the routines that leaders need to ascribe to are a major shift. The free flow of information and the ease of access to that information already mean that an organization's ability to control information has become limited. Yet, most organizations that I work with are still hesitant to open themselves up fully to their employees.

Cultural norms, routines, policies, and practices inhibit organizations from developing a culture of transparency. The impending result is a lack of confidence in your employees and a lack of trust in the organization. I'm not calling for organizations to throw everything on the table for full view of their employees, but there are things that you can easily do to start building a more transparent and adaptable organization.

Strategy is something that can and should be shared with the employees, and I mean more than just sharing the goals for the year. Employees should be made known of the major questions and strategic challenges facing the company. And a line of sight created to allow them to know how the role they have in the organization contributes to meeting those challenges. If you want to empower your people, allow them to help. Let them know what the big questions are that leaders are facing when making strategic decisions. Give your people insight and treat them like the professionals they are, and you'll be amazed by what you see.

Most organizations refuse to tell employees how they view them. Why? What are you hiding? How does it help? If you don't tell me how I'm viewed by the organization, then I'm left to make assumptions. As an employee, I could be right or wrong... but my next set of actions is based off that assumption. If I don't believe I'm valued, then I'm going to go elsewhere. The reality is that if I'm not highly valued, then my departure is a better move for all involved. But if I was truly valued? Then your silence has cost you my employment as a strategic asset. It's not a winning solution for you.

Other examples surely abound, but you need to start somewhere. It's a big change for most, and it will not be easy for some, but you have no choice in this day and age. Doing nothing is the first step in failing. Talent is moving to organizations they trust and organizations that empower them.

THE CULTURE REVOLUTION ISN'T BEING TELEVISED

It's a quiet revolution, a small step forward in how we think about organizations and the systems that we use to run them. It's a nod to the next generation; it's the culmination of technology disrupting the ways we work and how we think about work. There's a subtle transformation taking shape across corporate America. The idea that culture is more than just a billboard on a wall that celebrates the employee of the month. Culture is the new game. It's what attracts talent, it's what keeps people engaged, and it's what can make or break your company.

A misaligned culture will erode the foundation of any successful company. We talk about the practices and processes that are in play at most organizations that unknowingly undermine the organizational culture. We talk about what a high performing culture looks like. We talk about both the formal and informal cultures that exist within every culture. We do this because we truly believe that organizations live and breathe off the cultural nuances that pervade organizations.

There are some fundamental truths of what makes a good culture, but the reality is that the culture in each organization is unique. It's what makes the work so fascinating. The base element may be the same: empowered workers in a trusting environment that are given the freedom to make an impact, but the way this gets defined in each organization varies tremendously. It's the way the policies, the structures, and the people interact to form the unique blend of culture in any office.

CHAPTER 4

Helping Your Employees Contribute their Best

Are we putting our best people in the best spots? Once we figure out what we have for talent, do we have the people in the organization that will help us meet our business strategy? Then we have to figure out how skilled they are. If we're not committed to putting the best people in the best spot for their success, then can we really say we're driving toward success in our business strategy? Part of thinking about deployment is how to move the chess pieces around on the chessboard. How do we make sure we have people where they need to be? The biggest challenge we find often is talent mobility.

There was an organization I worked for before I started my consulting firm, where we talked about the four steps for really deploying talent around the organization.

KNOW who the talented people are. Who they are, what they want, what they need, what allows them to be successful, why they stay with the company? We need to know things about them. Once we've done that, we can understand the difference in their talent needs and knowledge, skill, and ability, and what we have as requirements in the organizations.

Whenever there is a gap between the talent and demonstrated skills, we need from them versus what they have, we need to **GROW** those skills.

Then we need to **SHOW** these talented people across the organization in a way that we really showcase, not only their contributions but also who they are to the organization. How they came into the organization, what are some of the things they have done that makes them exemplary?

How do we **FLOW** them where they need to go? The whole idea of flowing people is if we're truly committed to the organization becoming successful, we won't see a lot of hoarding of talent. There are famous instances where managers, who have been successful with teams, will have this group of top talent but they will hold them to the point of stunting their growth and movement through the organization because they feel that they won't be successful without those people working directly for them.

Talent deployment only works in an organization where leaders are committed to moving top talent around, giving them the best opportunities to be successful.

It wasn't very long ago when the big way to move into leadership positions was with job rotation programs. In the early 2000s, just before the start of the 2010s, that went away. There was this feeling that rotational job programs weren't helpful because people wouldn't be there long enough to learn and contribute. I think that now we're starting to see a return to that. Rotational assignments of 18 months can give a new employee a great perspective of the organization and is one of the best ways to engage the Millennial and Gen Z population.

Baby Boomers might not like that or think there wasn't enough time to settle in, learn the routine, and be comfortable, and for Baby Boomer leaders it wasn't enough time to get to know an employee or build trust. Gen Xers and Millennials are more agreeable to rotational assignments because they want to see more and are more excited by changing the scenery.

Rotational assignments, cross-functional projects, things of that nature, have a substantial benefit to organizations since they bring opportunity to move talent around, show that talent off, grow them into what needs to be done, and allows more of the organization to know who these talented people are. That is a lot of help to engagement and retention because people get to see them work and the value of the employee to the organization goes up.

Is the contribution of each employee to the overall mission very clear? Is your best talent focused on the most important activities or are they just hanging around? Are there certain jobs and projects considered developmental roles that we should flow top talent into, Gen Xer or Millennial, and really allow them to contribute? What happens when there's a person in a stretch assignment sinking instead of swimming? How do we rescue them?

One thing a good friend of mine said when asked why she stayed with the same organization for 25 years, was that she's worked for the same employer for 25 years, but she's had multiple jobs. She had the opportunity to do many things, and that allowed her to stay and have not only a job but also a long career.

Deploying Talent by Generation

Our Traditionalists are retiring, but when you think about how you would deploy them, they're very stable, detail oriented, thorough, loyal, and hard working. Where would you want those attributes?

The Baby Boomers are very service oriented, driven, really want to please, and are good team players. Where would you want them? Customer-facing positions, sales positions. You don't have to teach a Baby Boomer those skills because they're born into it.

Gen X is super adaptable, technology literate, very independent, not intimidated by authority, and very creative. A good fit for innovating, entrepreneurial positions. Maybe starting up a new business line or product line. They can go it alone, working without having a lot of supervision. Every company I've ever worked with or consulted with often talks about wishing that they had employees that didn't need hand-holding. Gen X is born with these skills.

Millennials believe in collective action and optimism. They have very high tenacity and a heroic spirit. They love multitasking and are not just technology literate, but technology savvy. They're digital natives. When you think about those characteristics, how might you deploy Millennial?

Are we matching generational characteristics to the positions people are coming into to set everyone up for the best possible outcome?

If you're in the business of leading others, you have a responsibility to help the process along. We know that motivation is an intrinsic drive for each individual. It's not something that we can create or force unto others, but as leaders, it's our responsibility to identify with our teams as individuals and to learn about what motivates each of them to succeed. By doing this, you can shape a culture of purpose by helping others tap into what's purposeful and meaningful to them. There's an upfront commitment of time and energy from you to make this happen, and it isn't something to rush through. If your motivation is to rush through the process, don't even start it, it will backfire. There will be bumps along the road and times when business demands take you in a different direction. Motivation gets sapped, purpose gets lost, it happens to all of us.

Your goal as the leader is to minimize those hiccups. It's to find the bigger picture and link back to the underlying purpose, beliefs, and values that your employees hold dear. One of my number one rules of leadership is getting out of the way. Let people work, let them bring forth passion, energy, and drive. Let them show you excitement. Your job is to help shepherd them along, it's not to leash them and pull them along with you. If you want engaged and productive workers, give them a purpose. Help them find the meaning in what they do. Make it personal for them.

The idea that we don't bring our personal selves to the office is bull. Work is very personal, we're not machines. Every interaction that we have is on a personal level, and emotions are shared through an open loop system. They're contagious. If you want to sit back and act like you don't give a shit, by all means, you have every right to do that, but remember that it trickles down. Remember that those around you see it, feel it and start to mimic it. If you can't find purpose in your work, and if you can't get behind your people, it's time to get unstuck and look for a new job. We spend too much of our waking hours working to not feel good about what we do.

COACHING FOR PERFORMANCE

If you want performance out of your people, it's time that you start coaching them. Engage them, encourage them, and reward them. Provide them with the tools that they need to make an impact in the organization. Talk with them about what your vision is, give tips on how to succeed in the organization and then get of the way.

Let them do their thing but don't disappear on them. Be there to provide the right guidance when needed. Perhaps most importantly, you need to know when to step away. Become adept at reading your people. If done wisely, your coaching sessions can replace your performance management conversations. It's unlikely that you'll be able to sway your company to drop performance management completely, so it's important that you set proper expectations with your people.

Not every coaching conversation should be a part of the formal performance record. You need to create a space where employees understand that coaching isn't a form of discipline and that it isn't something that will always land in the formal record. That being said, it's also important to make it clear that if the guidance provided in some of the coaching sessions continues to go unheeded, and performance continues to dip, it may very well become a part of the formal performance process.

Coaching is a balance between art and science. You don't want to appear that you're micro-managing your people, but you don't want to leave them in the wilderness. To become a good coach, you should think about the dynamics at play that include the culture of the organization, the business goals and objectives, the interpersonal relationships and the hard science of how to get results in a competitive environment.

This is your team, it's time to step up and coach, then get out of the way and let them do their thing.

The Only Constant Is Change

"The only constant is change, continuing change, inevitable change that is the dominant factor in society today." - Isaac Asimov

It feels to me like this holds true in the workplace, particularly in how we constantly look to institute new structures, new processes and new innovations in the hope that it gives us an edge over our competitors. I have seen organizations introduce the newest and greatest management theory only to replace it a few months later with another idea. I have seen CEOs turnover frequently in organizations and each time one leaves, another one comes in to implement their change agenda.

I'm not making a case that change is bad, but for change to be sustainable, it needs to become a habit. We have been so inundated with the idea and the practice of change that we have become used to the idea that something will not stick. So, we automatically resist it. The irony is that we are so wired for change, that we don't let the change play out because we expect it to fail or to get swept up in the tide of change and get pushed out before it even gets started. Every time that you roll an initiative out that doesn't stick, you undermine the chance of the next actually working. Real change requires new habits to be formed.

The Intersection of People and Tasks

Good leadership and good management are all about matching the right people with the right tasks. It's really about what weight you give to each and how you balance the push and pull of both in an organization. If you want to be a good leader, you focus on people and the systems that support them. If you want to be a good manager, you focus on the tasks, their interdependencies across an organization and how they align with the overall business strategy. If you want to be a great manager and leader, you focus on both and determine what levers to pull and when.

To be great, you need to learn how to scan your environment and keep an eye on what pressures are impacting your people. You need to understand how the systems operate, the policies that dictate the way work gets done and how people interact. The balance of being a great leader and manager comes into play when decisions need to be made that impact both. It becomes a balance when you have to implement policies that impact the people but benefit the tasks.

It's about understanding the downstream impacts on your people and anticipating the reactions and behaviors that will result. Conversely, it's also about how to navigate decisions about people that impact tasks, and the way work gets done. Balancing the two is what differentiates good from great. The workplaces that we operate in are vastly different than it used to be, but the basic tenants of good leadership and management still hold true. In the end, it's ultimately about the intersection of people and tasks.

What Happened to Integrity in Leadership?

As a result of the presidential campaign season of 2012, I became a big supporter of Politifact.com as a resource. I would check the site regularly because it felt like half of what was being said by both parties was either a blatant lie or twisted accusation. It has always been this way in some form or another, but now we are so inundated with information that it is hard not to notice it.

Political elections are supposed to be about core values. When I think about core values, the first that comes to my mind is integrity. It matters in leadership. Unfortunately, we have created a system based on sound bites and quick hitting verbal assaults. We like the one-liner and a good zinger, but as leaders, this isn't realistic. It doesn't provide context and doesn't enable people to understand the full account of what has happened.

The details are critical elements to any story; we need to be able to speak the truth in our politics, our boardrooms, and our offices. We need people to stand up for integrity. Without it, there is no trust, and without trust, there is no real communication. Beyond the political realm, take a look at what has recently happened in the Citigroup Boardroom with Vikram Pandit. A day after announcing corporate earnings, Vikram Pandit resigned after a boardroom clash. Millions of dollars of investment decisions were just made the day before based on the implied trust that Pandit would continue to lead the company and build for a better future. It didn't happen. He bailed. But why?

Early indications are a lack of trust from within the boardroom. They had seen enough of Pandit, which is their prerogative, but it brings to question their integrity when both parties knowingly go into the earnings call and act as if nothing is happening. Investors depend on reliable and accurate information to make decisions, and this impacts too many people. Leaders need to step up and act with integrity when so much is on the line -- politically or financially, because integrity matters.

Allowing Your Employees to Own Their Career Success

The big picture of owning your own succession plan is figuring out what your plan should be to achieve your desired career success without losing your authentic self.

With the changes the economy has gone through the past couple of years, many organizations now know that they have to change the way they think. It's not an industrial-age business environment anymore. You can't treat employees today like factory workers. You can't hire a superstar as the one person that's going to fix your organization and make it all better. It's about team building.

That's a cliché, and I hated hearing it used over and over in meetings, but it really is about building a team-based leadership structure. Everyone's a brick in the wall. Every individual and organization as an entity has their own personality and ego, but it's a collective ego, a collective culture. By understanding both—defining and then examining the best way to make things work better.

The culprit responsible for many of the problems we face as individuals and organizations are society's need and demand for instant satisfaction and instant gratification in all aspects of life—especially careers. Nothing of real value in life comes from simply pushing a button to obtain.

There is no button that you can push to simply get unstuck. Being stuck in the middle isn't only something that happens to an individual. Some organizations are stuck between a '70s mindset of how to run their business — monolithic and hidebound – and the needs of today's multigenerational, virtual working, work-life balance demanding, and individuals.

For Gen Xers, we no longer want to be tied to a desk in the corporate office for 60 hours a week. We no longer want to put on our corporate uniform (a business suit is still a uniform) and troop off to drab tan cubicle farm, or a row of sterile offices just like our Baby Boomer colleagues have every day for decades–like lemmings going off of a career cliff. The workplace today is very different, and there are numerous diverse dynamics at play above and beyond just generational difference.

As an individual, you can't constantly live off of the organization feeding you the line, "You have a lot of opportunities here." If the opportunity doesn't show up, you're spinning your wheels. If you're being told, "In five or ten years, you'll get that shot," that's hard to swallow. Do you want to spend what could be one-quarter of the years you have left hoping for career success? Do you want to deny your career passion simply because it may be different than anything you have done professionally to this point?

Assuming you're around 40 years old, ten years could be one-quarter of your living years and one-half of your viable (remaining) career working years. Organizations need to understand that it's with this perspective that some Gen Xers are thinking and rethinking their career choices. Organizations need to begin planning for this shift in thinking as they bring practice to their talent management philosophy if they expect to retain top talent. "Wait and see" isn't a career strategy when the gift of tomorrow is guaranteed to no one.

Are Your Leaders Being Worked Around?

Are there people in your office that you would rather not work with? I don't mean because you don't like them personally, but they stonewall initiatives. They're roadblocks to work, or they refuse to offer any help when it comes down to getting things done. They would rather pull out the job description and tell you that they're really sorry that they cannot help but, unfortunately, it isn't in their job description.

Do this enough times, and I'm sure you'll start to dislike them personally. But what's most likely is that you'll learn to work around them. Working around people is a clear sign of a dysfunctional team. It's an indication that you have an informal network in play. In and of itself, it isn't bad, but in this type of situation; it's clearly the result of negative behaviors.

When it becomes commonplace for people on your team to say that it's easier to do it myself than it is to work with that person, you clearly have some coaching to do. Hopefully, it isn't you the leader that they're working around. If it is, then you're leading your team in title only. If you start to see patterns where people would rather beg for forgiveness than ask for permission when working with you, take it as a clear sign that they're not buying what you're selling. Is it that they don't trust in what you're asking them to do, or is it that they don't see it as a viable solution to the problem at hand?

This is office politics. It happens every day, in every company. The question that you need to ask yourself as a leader is whether or not you're in the way of getting work done. Are you the reason that the politics are being played? Are you the reason that dysfunctional teams are running around the building?

It's time to get introspective and start asking yourself the harder leadership questions. Are you the problem?

Checking All the Boxes

I was coaching someone, and we started talking about visionary leadership. We were looking at her 360 results, and it was pretty clear to me that she had a good grasp of who she was and how others responded to her. Her directs were big fans, and her bosses seemed really pleased with what she had accomplished up to this point. The one thing that kept popping up was her lack of visionary leadership. Her group recently underwent a massive shift. Roles were realigned, people were maligned, and feelings still lingered. She was given control of a small team. It was evident in the feedback that her team was supportive. She started to address all concerns early on and often. She brought issues to the table, aired them out and worked as a team to solve them. She prides herself on never assigning something to her team that she wouldn't do.

Things were working, the team started to hum. She talked about the long-term state and what the team and work would look like once they got through all of this. They celebrated wins and put to bed old habits. She followed the script for change to the letter. But the one recurring piece of constructive feedback was (the perception of) her lack of visionary leadership. Something was wrong. We talked through the steps and the actions, what she was doing, what was working, what was resonating and I asked her to describe for me the end state. It sounded very reasonable, but when we dug a little deeper, that is where it stopped. It was reasonable. It made sense, but it didn't necessarily inspire. She was in a space where she could get her head around the idea.

Her team understood the direction and was up to follow, but they didn't feel the passion. They were missing the inspirational messaging. They knew she was committed but didn't know how inspired she was about the idea. To me listening in, it felt like the path was dictated to her, out of her control and influence. So she made the most of it, put together a detailed plan and went along for the ride. But she never put the brakes on to find the inspiration to compel her team to new heights. She had checked all the boxes, but one necessary emotional intelligence component was a glaring omission.

Career Patience or Success: A Personal Choice

Baby Boomers like to preach patience when it comes to talking about career moves and opportunities. These "old school" leaders want employees to soak in their roles before they consider them for the next opportunity. They like to ensure proper protocols are met and that succession is done pragmatically. But it isn't about the leader. It isn't about proper processes and procedures. It isn't about the policies. It is about the employee and about the business.

In today's workplace, there isn't much time left to be patient. Don't misread me as saying that career decisions should be hasty, or that we should all become serial career jumpers, but there are some people who should be targeted for fast-track promotions, and there are some policies (and leaders) currently in place that get in the way of doing what's best for the business. Success doesn't always follow a linear path of progression.

The people to fast-track are those individuals who display high levels of ability, aspiration, and engagement. They're the ones who are not going to be patient. If you want to keep them, you better find challenging opportunities for them. Don't hold them back just because your HR policies say that you cannot do skip level promotions, or that you cannot give a raise of more than three percent. That is utter nonsense.

The moment that a talented person walks out of the door for lack of challenging opportunities, your organization loses. Realize now that the organization will pay as much as two times the salary of the departing employee to hire, train, and gain production from the new employee as their replacement. And then there is no guarantee that this person will be a fit with the culture. HR departments should be helping organizations think about their employees as strategic assets.

We need to create better systems to retain our people. Telling a talented Gen Xer, or an ambitious Millennial to bide their time and wait in line will not sit well with them. It's the equivalent of saying wait and hope for the best. Hope isn't a strategy when it comes to career success. You must seek and find the career of your dreams with both passion and resiliency. There are opportunities out there for your best people, believe it.

I enjoy talking to my contacts that are executive recruiters because networking isn't a spectator sport. I stay "in the know" about the status of the market for top talent, and it's still very intense. Top talent is in demand and has options. Those options will "pay" your top talent a lot more walking in the door to get them than you would even think of paying to keep them.

I use the concept of "pay" metaphorically to mean challenging, rewarding work for an appreciative leader. This is the new pay raise that top talent employees are seeking in a post-2008 recession economy. If we want our businesses to innovate, then it's time that we start being innovative with our talent pipeline. We need to critically examine our restrictive policies and procedures. It's a brave new workplace out here, and either "old school" leaders get it or organizations will get left behind.

Networking: Givers, Takers, and Matchers

Networking in today's workplace may be more important than it has ever been. You have to take a broad perspective and start building a bigger network. Work no longer gets done in a vacuum. It gets done through a multi-layered and complex web of individuals and entanglements. At the heart of that web lie both personal relationships and interactions.

There's a great book by Adam Grant called *Give and Take*. I'm not going to go into all of the detail here, but it's a great book by a great young mind. He talks about interpersonal dynamics and creates a view of three types of people. Givers, takers and those in the middle, the matchers.

The givers are the people who would do anything to help a colleague, a friend, and even a stranger. Takers are those that take from others. They view relationships based on what they can get out of them. They look to impress influencers, and they trample on those they see as less influential. Then there are matchers. They're the people in the middle. Those who may have been burned as a giver or a reformed taker. They look at relationships in some ways as transactional. They do for you; you do for them.

The biggest takeaway for me is that it's actually the givers, with the right guardrails in place that makes the most effective employee in today's workplace. They're the ones outperforming their peers, they're the ones using their relationships to help navigate complex organizational structures, and they're the ones who have learned a key dynamic of interpersonal relationship building. Givers are willing to pay options forward. At all times. They stop asking for help for themselves (within reason), and they look for ways to help others in their network. They constantly look for opportunities to bring people together, they look for ways to network people across boundaries, across function and they help put together teams that can solve problems or launch initiatives.

As the workplace grows more integrated, more complex, and the pace of work continues to accelerate, you'll need to learn how to navigate. Work can't be done alone anymore. In fact, the definition of work continues to change. What doesn't change is the fact that people need people. So take a moment to reflect, and think about which style should be yours.

MANAGING TRANSITIONS FOR DEVELOPMENT INSIDE THE ORGANIZATION

If you're in charge of development for your organization, what are you doing to manage transitions for your people? By transitions, I don't mean the exodus of folks out the door; I'm talking about how you manage people as they progress through their careers and transition into new roles. It's like watching a race car handle a hairpin turn. The ones that set up the turn right from the outset get to full speed faster than those that take the wrong preparation into the turn.

Many organizations we work with actively manage the transition from outside of an organization to inside an organization, but not the transition points for their internal employees. The assumption is that they've made it, they could promote to the next level, they understand how we operate, and they're ready to take on the next level. Unfortunately, more often than not, that's not the case.

There's a fundamental change of responsibilities, behaviors, and expectations as you promote into more senior roles. This takes preparation and diligence. It requires not only a behavioral shift but also a psychological one. If you're new to leading people, you can no longer rely on getting things done on your own. You have to learn to give up that mentality; you have to come to terms with allowing others to take on initiatives and to receive recognition for a job well done.

The biggest thing we see in organizations is an assumption that the workhorse individual contributor will make a good leader because they get things done. The biggest challenge for these folks is learning that they can't do it all alone, they need their team.

As employees promote into more senior roles, the challenge for many is working through what specific changes need to occur at each level for them to succeed. To be successful as you progress in your career, you need to learn how to give up control and how to broaden your focus beyond yourself, your immediate team, your group, or your function. Each transition requires that you scan the horizon more broadly and that you place yourself more thoroughly at the service of others. You become a leader not because of what you accomplish individually, but because of what you're able to get your team to accomplish with you.

Transitions at every level have a consequence and associated impact on the employee and to the organization. You can help manage these transitions by creating support mechanisms for your people. Training is one example, but it can't be the only solution. Most of the growing pains and learning that occurs happens on the job, you need to account for that and build flexible systems.

Flexibility with the framework is critical to implementation and utilization. The way you manage transitions should have aspects of standardization, but your tools have to flex for the level, the stage of transition, and the complexity of the role. Development that occurs in the classroom and is supported with on-the-job learning is most likely to succeed. Setting people up with tools that they can use to help move them along the curve of development is the first step.

The real rubber hits the road when the employee is back on the job. It's here that you need to equip employees and managers alike with the tools needed to succeed, learn and grow. Creating a knowledge management system or process is a step. It's a place where you can host information critical to each level of leadership. There's a host of offerings that you can provide, but here are the top five that we see work well in our client sites:

1. Coaches/mentors
2. Customized individual development plans
3. 360-degree feedback
4. Manager tool kits
5. Project-based learning

Every transition has an impact on your organization. Some positive, others negative, but regardless, the one thing we all know is that each transition also causes disruption to productivity.

How long that lasts and how deep it goes can be managed if you put the right processes and focus in place to support your people as they move through the organization.

Failure as an Innovation Strategy

Failure may be the world's greatest teacher, but in the corporate world, I've seen very little evidence of us paying much heed to it. We hear industry titans talk about failing all of the time. We hear them tell us that taking those early risks paid off in unimaginable ways, but in most corporate cultures there is very little tolerance for failure. Most organizations don't like to talk about failure, they don't challenge their people to try new things and take *smart* risks.

There is a clear difference between *smart* risks and risk for the sake of it. The distinction lies in the preparation phase and in the after action review. *Smart* risks are taken with proper thought and planning, there are mechanisms put in place to capture the learning in an attempt to understand what worked and what didn't. It's not a risk that is intentionally set up to fail, but the company goes in knowing that there's a good chance that it may fail. Employees leading the effort are prepped, they understand what's at stake, but they also should feel secure in the knowledge that if they do fail, the rewards for trying are greater than the penalties.

Too often we see organizations create cultures that cause inertia. The company says they want employees to push the envelope, but when reality hits, the employees know that the prudent thing to do is to sit back and continue with business as usual. They know failure can destroy or impede career progression. Why push it, when the easy thing to do is keep doing what's been done, make incremental progress, look busy and put some points on the board? This is what most organizations reinforce. They aren't creating cultures that view failure as an acceptable precedent for progress. They're killing the culture of innovation

Take a look at your structures and talk to your employees. Learn to let failure teach your organization, and you'll start to see progress. Failing fast can result in real-time innovation, and can drive employee engagement if leaders have a passion for success that is greater than their fear of failure.

CHAPTER 5

Helping Leaders Bridge Generational Gaps

How do you help multigenerational organizations look at the way their leaders interact with the different generations? Some specific differences need to be talked about, but some threads run through them all so we can have an organization that values, appreciates, and welcomes the different generational aspects.

How do we know what to have for each of the generations to grow and thrive in the organization? Let's think about what we've touched on. Engagement, talent acquisition, knowing what talent we're looking for, all leading to talent development. How do we develop the skills of any generation not only for today but tomorrow?

We've talked about retention and helping employees be their authentic self, which allows us to retain that top talent. The biggest challenge we see today is holding onto the top talent of the younger generations. In this chapter, we want to go about how we lead each generation. We'll take a deconstructive look at it.

TRADITIONALISTS (1)

We'll start with our Traditionalists, those folks who have been the builders of all of the organizations we have that we would call our Fortune 500. They're retiring and have changed their work preferences to reflect the economic downturn of 2008.

They're stable, detail oriented, thorough in their work, very loyal and hard working.

Leadership

They're less comfortable with jumping in on the fly. We can't rush onboarding for Traditionalists. We see Traditionalists returning to the workforce or changing where they show up because the 2008 downturn redefined retirement.

We want to show respect for their experience and help them believe the group is more important and powerful than just the individual. We don't want to make them feel that they're at the end of their use in an organization. This is the group that serves as the coach, mentor, or culture historian to help the teams of the day realize what the organization was like yesterday.

For our Traditionalists, the expectation should be spoken and written. It can't just be a hallway conversation. This cohort appreciates traditional formats, so no texts or abbreviations, but clear communication and setting rules and expectations. You tell them what you need to be done, and they'll do it with speed and efficiency. The best way to do that is to communicate any changes quickly. They thrive on not wasting time or effort and don't like ambiguity.

Take time to get to know them and respect their experiences. Don't mistake their silence for disinterest. They want a command and control style of management. Most importantly, evolve the team and set up a shared vision. This cohort, more than others, is very loyal to bosses and subordinates and always put the company first. The whole idea of the company man or company woman was born from this generation. They were brought up to value and trust authority.

Feedback

It needs to be clearly communicated, always a conversation forward. Not dwelling on any mistakes in the past, but moving forward to be better, do better, and be seen better by others. They need some praise from the team, so they see everyone is aware of their ability to be helpful. Even though this cohort might be at the end of their time, it doesn't mean they don't have aspirations. You want to show that you value their career and wisdom and look for opportunities to call on them for guidance and opinion.

Development

Should be immediate and clearly relevant to the use of their time. Invite them to participate in the discussion. Provide proper insight, giving them the opportunity to look at their peers or clients. Help them see this idea of development will be coming to them from someone who knows what they're talking about. They want an expert to show them what to do.

They enjoy coaching from someone of authority in the company. It has to be from someone who has achieved rank in a way that makes sense to the Traditionalist, that it's clear they have earned it.

Recognition

You want to celebrate the efforts of the team because this is a generation that believes in the team winning. Individual recognition will be good, but I recommend doing that in private while praising the team in public so everyone can share success. Be genuine. Issuing a personal thank you from the boss and a handshake certainly doesn't hurt. It's part of the foundation of how they do business. Recognize their achievements. Not just doing the job, but awards for going above and beyond.

BABY BOOMERS (2)

They're very service oriented and very driven to be successful, they're willing to go the extra mile. They want to please the leaders, please the organization and are good team players. As a leader, trying to assimilate into a team of Baby Boomers or a Baby Boomer into a team, you want to understand that they have a "whatever it takes" attitude. They want their time at work to be well spent, and this cohort actually lives to work. You want to be a visible, active, leader and take time to demonstrate how you have learned your role.

Leadership

Not unlike the Traditionalists, they want to see that their leaders are not just appointed, but have earned their position. Demonstrate that you have firsthand knowledge of the people who report to you, that you understand how they work and you have done the same job at some point. They really value chain of command, much like the Traditionalists, but this cohort is more "show me." They want you to show them that you understand the work up, down, and sideways. You're a leader, not just on knowledge, but also on ability.

There's a lot of talk about how to engage Millennials and Gen Xers, but little is being said about how to engage aging Boomers. They're at the sunset of their careers, which actually makes their level of engagement even more important.

Boomer managers and leaders are at the stage in their career where they're thinking about the legacy they will leave behind, the challenges they overcame and the success they accomplished. It may not be easy, but it's the right time to tap into this and use it to your company's advantage. You can take some fairly simple steps to make this happen.

1. Set up a coaching community for High Potentials
2. Create rotational assignments
3. Build a knowledge-sharing platform
4. Establish mentoring programs

You can appeal to ego and let them know they will indeed leave behind a legacy, that the torch needs to be passed and you're asking them to rise to one more challenge before they go. The coaching community would provide Boomers with the opportunity to work with high potential future leaders. You can structure it so that they're able to provide advice and consultation. If done right, it can even be an avenue for them to stay on with the organization after retirement in some nonemployee capacity.

For the rotational program, you should find younger employees who have the ability and aspiration for broader roles and move them under Boomers for short periods. The knowledge-sharing platform is a way to capture the knowledge that your Boomers have, and it enables them to continue to support and grow the company's legacy and culture. Lastly, you can create a formal mentoring program open to all employees that enable the Boomers to share their wisdom while simultaneously learning from others.

Goals

They want the top job and are always going to be focused on their path there. They're seeking the prestige of position and want increasing responsibility. That allows them to feel like they add value and that they have the opportunity to succeed. Some of the frustrations we have with Baby Boomers are that many times if their career stagnates, it's going to be tough for them to feel engaged or important. Goals should allow a certain amount of risk-taking. For them, work is an adventure. You want to hold them accountable for their actions and reward their work ethic. Nothing makes engagement easier for Baby Boomers than to create realistic goals and give them examples of what a good job looks like. You can really tap into the power motive for this generation.

Motivations

They want to excel in their careers, want to show they're on the path to the top job. They know the value of the 'we need you' mentality of the workforce. They want leaders to look at them and say we can't do without you. You'll retain them if you allow them to feel like they can be their authentic selves. You want to find ways where they can showcase their contributions.

Encourage celebrations within the team, as well as company-wide acknowledgments. When we think about the workforce that many organizations have, these are created by Baby Boomers. This is the cohort that carried forward the idea of the company picnic and giving benefits during the holiday season. They want the team to win, but they aren't shy about wanting to know who within the team is most helpful.

As a leader, we need to create an environment where ethics are important, even if in the news this is also the generation that has been challenged by financial ethics. There's a lot of that, they do value ethics and expect others to push back when not in agreement with them. They invite open discussion, open debate, and challenge people to share their thoughts and be willing to go to war for their ideas if they feel they're right.

Feedback

This cohort really values the face-to-face and the opportunity to be connected to their leader. As we move forward generationally, the tendency is to do everything electronically. Baby Boomers do a lot better with talking and giving that feedback firsthand.

Development

Help them build relationships they need the most. This cohort is ripe for help in the developing of soft skills, and their training should be competitive. We see in this generation the realization now that they've moved into leadership, is that their job is done with or through others. They're no longer doing the work, so they'll need soft skills on how to give feedback and delegate, how to influence without authority.

Give them an environment that allows for all levels of technical skill, so they don't feel intimidated as they learn, or feel inferior to Gen X and Millennial. They grew up with a lot of advancing technology, but they're not the digital natives like Millennials or tech literate like Gen X. If you're going to train them, you'll need to ask them questions. They have a lot of experience they can bring to the table and want a collaborate environment. Different from a traditional environment where the person in authority is allowed to be the sage on the stage. With Baby Boomers, they want to see the facilitation. Less instruction and more coaching of their knowledge and skill. When coaching this cohort, you really have to demonstrate your understanding of team goals. You don't want feedback to be written or email but told.

Recognition

For Baby Boomers, you want to recognize their achievements of moving up the ladder. They want someone to take the time and show that it is as much value to the organization as it is to them. You want that recognition to be public. They're big on trophies, plaques, pins, and such. Nothing says more to a Baby Boomer than the putting of a few extra dollars in their wallet as a testament to their achievement. Allow the Baby Boomer to really shine, the opportunity to rise through the ranks and demonstrate their worth by their achievements and progression.

GENERATION X (3)

Those were the particulars of our two senior generations. Now I'll talk about the gap that exists not only between the Baby Boomer and the Gen Xer but also between the Gen Xer and the Millennial. Those differences are noticeable, but they're ones that can be navigated. Gen X is very adaptable, technology literate, very independent, not intimidated by authority, and very creative. When you think about those aspects, it shows why this generation is the most entrepreneurial of the four generations. It's a challenge for managers to assimilate a Gen Xer into their team or lead Gen Xers, and you have to honor your commitment to them at all costs.

Leadership

Many times, our leaders fail to realize that their word means a lot to a Gen Xer. If you can't do it, be honest with your explanation on why it can't happen. You want to allow for flexibility in schedules and be willing to negotiate how and when work will get done. Allow them to take up the mantle of how and be flexible on the when and even the where the work gets done.

Much unlike the Baby Boomer who lives to work, this generation works to live. We see it as a vehicle to create the money needed to spend time and energy with family and friends on other pursuits. Giving the opportunity to negotiate schedule goes a long way to help a Gen Xer feel valued and be their authentic self. Much like the Traditionalists, you have to set clear objectives and allow them to have a plan, but you have to revisit that plan often. Make sure they're committed and working toward it. To let them drift can lead to disappointment with the leader if they don't know if there is any progress.

One of the hardest challenges of assimilating a Gen Xer onto a team is that Gen Xers are independent. Having hands-off supervision has to be earned, but they're going to work to earn that trust as much as they can. Micromanagement is stifling and suffocating to a Gen Xer. The quickest way to drive a Gen Xer into disengagement is not allowing them to get to a place of autonomy. Certainly, someone new to the organization will have to earn it, but the steps need to be clearly specified. There needs to be transparency about those opportunities.

You want to regularly review goals with your Gen X employees. You want to be sure that you're working to help them see what responsibilities they have. That deadlines are clearly communicated. You want to give them the opportunity to get their work done without interference or interruptions. The Gen Xer is working to live, so when they go to work, every moment is dedicated to meeting their goals. Interruption really drains Gen Xers. Those things need to be mitigated by leaders as much as possible. Nothing frustrates this generation more than the target they cannot hit. They're driven to check the box. The ever-elusive goal or arbitrary deadline can demoralize and disengage this generation.

For Gen Xers to be their authentic self, they should have a casual work environment. That doesn't necessarily mean casual dress, but people are allowed to refer to each other by first name and socializing is encouraged. Things of that nature are what Gen Xers want to see.

As a leader, you have to demonstrate to this cohort that it's okay and appreciated to work smarter and not harder. This is the first generation that doesn't think that the longer you're in the office, the more productive you are. They believe that you go into the office and do what you need to do.

They might go in for core hours, then go home and after the kids have gone to bed work for a few more hours. The office for them isn't the only place where work gets done. For them, the office is the place they go to interact with others to get work done. This is different from the older two generations. The Gen Xer is prone to starting work in a different time and place than others in the workforce. As leaders, we have to be mindful and show respect for that work style preference.

Goals

Gen X really appreciates leaders who keep us up to date and allows us to keep them up to date on career goals. We like that dialog. Gen Xers aren't afraid to ask for the development they think they need. While they might not be as driven as Baby Boomers to move up the ladder, Gen Xers like to know that whatever time they spend at work isn't only for them to complete the task at hand, but that they're investing in their ability to do more and have more.

This is a difference between that "be more, do more, have more" attitude of both Gen Xers and Baby Boomers. For a Generation Xer, it doesn't mean at your organization. It might be any organization. Sure, you might be the one giving them those opportunities, but recognize that to the Gen Xer, they see that as an opportunity to prepare themselves for the next twist or turn in their career journey. Allow them to be flexible, with numerous paths and options. Gen Xers really want the information to allow them to make choices in their career, and they like knowing that their career doesn't need to look like anyone else's to be deemed a success. Gen Xers don't like cookie cutter.

Motivations

Keep an ongoing dialog with their managers. Gen X votes with their feet concerning their manager's ability, success, and treatment of them. A Gen Xer will rather fake it until they can't, and then you'll find their two weeks' notice. They aren't going to get into a dialog of how you'll help them, they think as a leader you're supposed to know that, or if you're truly interested, you'll ask them about their wants. If you have leaders that don't do that, you'll lose talented Gen Xers, because they're waiting around for a leader to recognize what needs to be done to retain them or the best opportunity to depart the organization.

You need to create a clear progression map. As a generation, we expect to grow. We want to talk about what it means to stay with the organization. What's my three-year plan? What's my five-year plan? This is what Gen Xers think about. They don't want to risk spending their time and energy where they don't know if they can move up where they want.

You'll want to foster two-way communications with your Gen X employees. It has to be a dialog. Gen Xers don't like to be told what to do. They want to engage in conversation, and you want to clearly communicate and connect strategy to the big picture. It has to be less about, "I'm the leader, and I told you to do this," but more creating a line of sight for Gen Xers. Let them see how what they do today adds value, how their place in the organization helps it achieve its business strategy. By doing that, you appeal to the heart, head, and wallet of a Gen Xer.

Feedback

Gen Xers trust the employer's time management skills and for this cohort checking with them regularly but not frequently is the way to go. They're fine getting coaching at the weekly or biweekly meeting. This cohort appreciates having a clear plan, but not micromanagement. It's a thin line to walk. Feedback and coaching need to be regular, but if it's too regular and too pointed, it becomes micromanagement. Focus on coaching and development and how it's going to build their career portfolio. This generation believes that the skills they're learning have wheels and handles on them that can be taken and moved as they go on their career journey. If you can focus on that, you can drive their engagement.

Development

To develop our Gen Xers, we want to include leaders and peers and demonstrate a commitment to their development. We want to promote new ideas on how to get things done. If they come up with a new way to do things, we need to let them have an opportunity to demonstrate that. We want to find projects that foster their creativity and entrepreneurial side. The biggest thing that jazzes a Gen Xer is telling them what needs to be done, why it needs to be done when it needs to be done, and then allowing them to run wild with creating a solution. A 'long memory' culture, or buttoned up culture, stifles the innovative spirit that naturally comes along with the Gen Xers in your workforce. If your culture doesn't value innovation or always does what it's always done, realize you're setting yourself up for challenges with your Gen Xers that might lead to lack of engagement and retention problems.

Recognition

Offer variety. Allow them to choose from a list of options that have equal value. This cohort isn't always tied to money. They might like more free time, more vacation time, or more work from home. That flexibility can really increase retention.

Express gratitude for their contributions in private. Gen Xers don't want to fuss over how we do our jobs in public. We just like to know that our leader can see what we're doing and is appreciative. Gen Xers love to have leaders who appreciate their hobbies and passions outside of work. They like to know that their leaders appreciate them as people first and employees second. Many Gen Xers feel frustration for working with Traditionalists and Baby Boomers, and that they're seen by these generations as just employees and a means to an end. Reality is, you can get a Gen Xer to be much more engaged if you see them and allow them to see that you see them as a person who has a weekend, who has a family. If you can do that, you can expect solid business results from this generation.

MILLENNIALS (4)

So you see the gaps, the differences, the shifting needs, and desires of the generations, and that brings us to the Millennials or Generation Y. This is the cohort that is entering the workforce more and more. This cohort is often the most baffling to the other three generations because they show up so differently than what you see between a Gen Xer and a Boomer, and certainly between a Boomer and a Traditionalist. They bring a collective action way of thinking. They're very optimistic, very tenacious, they have a heroic spirit, and they're very good at multitasking. Technological savvy is something they're born with.

Leadership

As a leader, you want to make sure you demonstrate a sincere interest in the individual. Take time to get to know the goals and personality of each of your employees regardless of their generational cohort.

The Gen Xer wants to be recognized for their experience and what they've achieved out of work. They want their leader to let them feel like they're known. You want to take time and really set aside onboarding for this cohort. Not just make it part of their workday, but allow them to see the transition between work and onboarding. Have clear delineation in the activities you're putting in front of them.

As a leader, we want to articulate how their working for you will help them achieve their personal goals and at the same time achieve the company goals. This cohort likes work that will make them look good, make the organization look good, and make the leader look good. This is similar to Traditionalists. They also believe in making their boss look good. Millennials are different; they will work hard to make their boss look good if they know it will make them look good. You want to outline the steps they need to do to achieve a goal. This is a cohort that appreciates directive leadership. Do this, and then do this, then do that. They want to be told how. That's one of the biggest differences between a Gen Xer and a Millennial. Gen Xers want to figure it out on their own. Millennials want to know how you want that done so they can please you, and follow it by the letter so they'll have your favor and recognition.

You want to establish check-ins along the way to document progress and provide frequent feedback. It can be done formally in meetings, but also by what I like to call "the morning drive by," where you stop by their desk to check in and see what's going on. Just socializing and managing by walking around is big with this generation.

Goals

Millennial and Gen Z employees benefit from knowing that what they're learning right now will help them in the future, and are very open to asking about how to move up. They aren't necessarily impatient, but they're insistent. Autonomy, just like with Gen X, is important. The organization needs to realize they're very focused on what's in it for them. The way you can get a Millennial to feel that their time is worthwhile is to put a career path with clear milestones in place and identify those people whom they can talk with to confirm their career movement.

Motivations

Feedback is a key motivator. Constant feedback. Expect that they'll engage in career discussions with you. They feel that they have a lot to give; they feel they have a life that has allowed them to have greater perspective in the same amount of time because of technology and how fast the world moves.

They want mentors giving them social activities and building communities. Friends and network are important. You want to encourage in work activities, to come in and work with others, play with others, in the context of being in line with the organization so they can be their authentic selves.

To many, this generation is very needy, when in fact to some they're demonstrating more engagement than the other generations. You want to leverage those strengths. This cohort prefers to work on their own terms, much like Gen X, but the difference is that they want more immediate, hands on. It's why many Gen Xers have a hard time leading Millennials. Baby Boomers have an easy time because it's more like their children. Gen Xers struggle with what's seen as an incessant need.

Feedback

Millennials want feedback from everyone, not just their leaders. For some leaders, it might be challenging to lead Millennials because they won't only talk to you about what they could be doing differently. They have no problem talking with others and aren't afraid of feedback. The challenge is that not everyone who gives feedback is always looking for the Millennials best interest.

With coaching, you want to be positive, and when you give them constructive feedback, be prepared to give them a 2:1 ratio of positive to constructive. This cohort is made up of the children of helicopter parents and a generation where everyone wins, and there are no hard feelings. Very different from how Gen Xers were raised. They were told there is one winner and everyone else is second place, and to expect more constructive feedback than confirming.

Development

You want to involve the whole cohort and create experiences that are interactive and fun. You want everyone to take a role in some part of the development, teaching, or training process. Offer and commit to developing their skills, they see the time they're spending with your organization as on the road to where they're going. They see it as getting them ready to go somewhere else. They like constant feedback, and the best practice with their cohort is to ask them a question they often heard in school. What did you learn today? Is there anything you think I need to know? They love to have that dialog and have that connection. Ask them what they've learned, seen, or feel could be done differently.

Recognition

They cherish their individuality. They love to have their successes celebrated publicly and being seen as having done a good job by leaders and peers. Their constructive feedback is definitely done in private with this cohort. Saving of face is important for them.

You want to offer top learning opportunities. You want to establish a culture where those who go above and beyond have a chance to stand out. Employee of the month parking space or similar rewards. They want to know that others see them as having taken the initiative and propelled themselves toward their goals.

***

There's a lot here about how we need to lead across generations, and how organizations can see what needs to be done really get business results from a multigenerational workforce. What percentage of your organization's leaders spends 30% of their time or more on talent issues? Are leaders developed internally or being brought in from outside?

Organizations should look at the success rate of developed versus acquired leaders. Are leaders being held accountable for talent across the different generations? Which percentage of leader compensation is dedicated to developing other leaders? Which leaders have an excellent reputation for developing other leaders? That question has higher implications above all others. Leaders who are seen as developers will have the most value to your organization because they have figured out how to flex their leadership style to get the best results, regardless of which generation they're from, or which generation they're working with. You want them to build the knowledge, skill, and ability for the future by taking a good inventory of the current knowledge, skill, and ability and the employees that demonstrate that. You need to hold onto and hold up those leaders and single them out privately as the ones who are key and hold critical roles in driving your business to success.

GENERATION Z (5)

Northeastern University is the leader of the conversation on Generation Z. The following infographic (used with their permission) is from their 2014 national survey on higher education

Not to be confused with a "Millennial" as a person reaching young adulthood around the year 2000, Generation Z, as they have been coined, comprises those born in 1996 or later. Generation Z (also known as Post-Millennials, the iGeneration, Founders, Plurals, or the Homeland generation) is the demographic cohort that follows the Millennials. This generation makes up 25.9% of the United States population, the largest percentage, and contributes $44 billion to the American economy. By 2025, they will account for half of the U.S. population.

Today the word relevant is continually being refined, and Gen Z lives in a workplace of continuous updates. Gen Z processes information faster than other generations thanks to apps like Snapchat and Vine. Thus, their attention spans might appear to the untrained eye to be significantly lower than Millennials. As someone who spends a lot of time with Generation Z in my role as a Business School Professor, my experience would suggest that their attention span is actually more advanced.

It's easy to look at Gen Z's addiction to social media with cynicism, but it's more productive to use their desire for recognition to your advantage. If they want a good pat on the back or to be recognized in front of the group for their hard work, give it to them! And do it even if the recognition is for smaller tasks. The point is not precisely what they are working on—the point is to help them feel great about the work they're doing, even when they are at the entry level.

Many Gen Z identifying factors can be traced back to the recession in 2008, from their frugality to their value of experiences, and increased likelihood to become entrepreneurs. With hints of a pending recession, could this be a signal that loyalty is a nonstarter? This fall, another crop of Gen Z college grads will hit the workforce. And from experience again, the most crucial thing that separates this cohort from their Millennial forbearers is found in their expectations of the workplace.

Graduating amid the worst economic crisis since The Great Depression with the memory of 9-11 fresh in their minds, Millennials (and many of us Gen Xers, as well) carry a nonspecific sense of dread about our economic and social conditions. They and we toiled during a dour moment in the country's history, one where we were told that recovery would be slow, that we should be happy just to have a job, and that we probably would not enjoy the same quality of like our parents did.

Gen Z did most of its growing up during a time of unprecedented growth—couched in the recovery that led to a current streak of 94 consecutive months of job creation. They've heard the horror stories from their older siblings, but the reality for them has been the opposite. To manage them, leaders must keep this context in mind. The freedom these workers feel manifests in their work decisions. This is a shared trait with Millennials, who are famously generalized as "following their passion" in their work. The reality of the working world may also set in when Gen Z enters the workforce, they often realize it is not their real passion, see the dead-end for the first time, and reevaluate their career path. It's not about the salary.

Accepting that no work conditions are ideal, Gen Z is attracted to opportunities where they do what they want. Good managers must foster this instinct, and point it in constructive directions. Make each task mean something; illustrate for them how to see the big picture, and outline how their role is helping it become realized. Managers are to be reminded that work with a sense of purpose is paramount to engaging the Gen Z employee. An opportunity and the empowerment to contribute early and often is what this generation is seeking from their leaders in the workplace.

Gen Z wants to their path to success from day one. Managers can empower them in small, safe ways by enabling them with tasks to own now, and tasks to aspire to as part of a personal development plan that is reviewed regularly. That will allow them to see their path of growth in the organization in a highly tangible way.

Generation Z has also come of age in the shadow of Millennials who prize hyper-competence (or at least the appearance of it), which, in my experience so far, has manifested in a strong desire to learn. Specifically, I have noticed that recent grads are less likely to think they "know everything" and are instead keenly interested to know more. More than the preceding generation—or my generation—they are seeking opportunities to add or sharpen skills. Leaders should not at all be surprised to be asked by their Gen Z employee for "their story." This generation learns best through the story of the human experience. Gen Z takes this into the workplace and seeks to connect with their coworkers and leaders on a human level. The story of how a leader got to where they are now is motivating to the Gen Z employee to show them how there is no one correct path to personal career success.

This is a generation that wants to change the world and has definitive ideas about how to do it. Instead of quashing this youthful enthusiasm, leaders need to embrace it by showing them the impact of their daily efforts and look for ways to foster their passions, even if it's outside of their job description. Mentorship, cross-functional training, and leadership storytelling can go a long way in attracting, engaging and keeping this dynamic cohort that is joining the workforce.

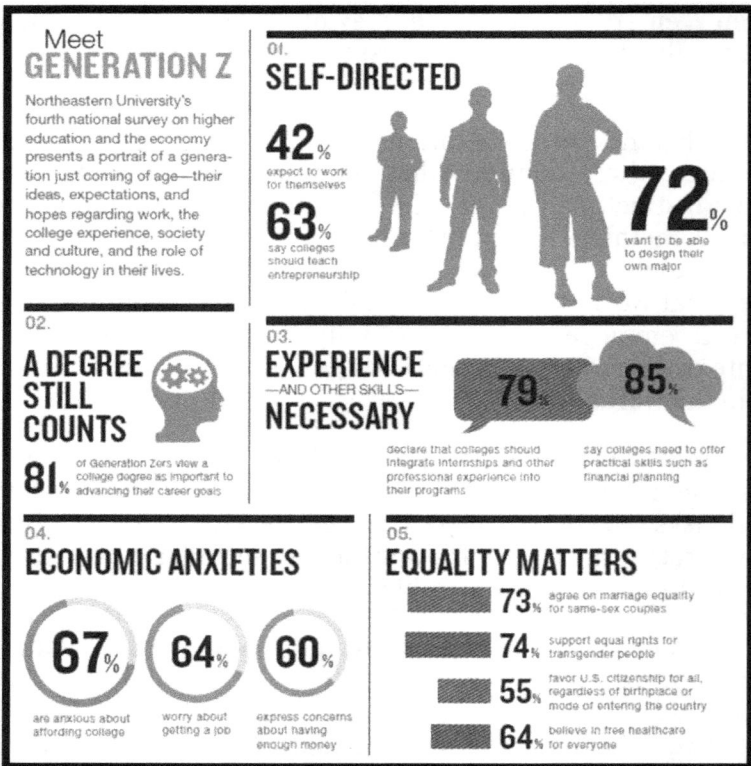

Meet
GENERATION Z

Northeastern University's fourth national survey on higher education and the economy presents a portrait of a generation just coming of age—their ideas, expectations, and hopes regarding work, the college experience, society and culture, and the role of technology in their lives.

01.
SELF-DIRECTED

42% expect to work for themselves

63% say colleges should teach entrepreneurship

72% want to be able to design their own major

02.
A DEGREE STILL COUNTS

81% of Generation Zers view a college degree as important to advancing their career goals

03.
EXPERIENCE
—AND OTHER SKILLS—
NECESSARY

79% declare that colleges should integrate internships and other professional experience into their programs

85% say colleges need to offer practical skills such as financial planning

04.
ECONOMIC ANXIETIES

67% are anxious about affording college

64% worry about getting a job

60% express concerns about having enough money

05.
EQUALITY MATTERS

73% agree on marriage equality for same-sex couples

74% support equal rights for transgender people

55% favor U.S. citizenship for all, regardless of birthplace or mode of entering the country

64% believe in free healthcare for everyone

Northeastern University - northeastern.edu/innovationsurvey

102

Here are some of the defining characteristics I've seen in Generation Z from my observation as a Generation X parent, and a member of the workforce. Keep in mind, that while based on small sample size, these attributes are most often on display:

- Generation Z is Skeptical: They tend to be more realistic not idealistic, seemingly world-weary from the tough economy, asymmetrical terrorism, and complexities of life.
- Generation Z is Introverted: Perhaps because they watched their older siblings get in trouble from posting controversial content on social media, but younger teens don't want to be tracked. Apps like Snapchat and Whisper have seen explosive Gen Z growth in the last few years. In contrast, Facebook has lost 25 percent of that demographic since 2011.
- Generation Z is Entrepreneurial: Like Millennials, these students plan to be pioneers, not merely settlers, in their careers. 72% of current high school students want to start a business. They know life is hard and requires work.
- Generation Z is Hyper-Active: By almost every measurement so far, they take multitasking to a new level. They prefer to be on multiple screens at once, not two like Millennials. Get ready to communicate to them as they look around, but not into your eyes.
- Generation Z is Technology-Enabled: If we thought Millennials were addicted to technology, this generation is far more. In surveys, these teens put technology in the same category as air and water. They cannot imagine living without being connected all the time.

In 2015, Generation Z comprised the largest portion of the U.S. population, at nearly 26%; edging out Millennials (24.5%), and the generation is estimated to generate $44 billion in annual spending. To nail down the demographics on Generation Z in the United States, I consider this generation to span the years of 1995 to 2010 with the oldest of this generation turning 21 years old this year. Some are worried about being able to afford a college education. And those that do manage to pay (through educational loans and other support) are coming out of college, highly concerned about student debt and faced with a growing income gap and a shrinking middle-class. This all has led to increased stress levels for them and their families.

Their concerns go beyond personal and national economics. The oldest members of Generation Z were around 6 years old when the 9/11 attacks occurred meaning that there have been significant events in their young lives, which have resulted in a feeling of unsettlement and insecurity about the environment—the world—in which they were raised and will occupy as adults.

According to Forbes, in 2015 Generation Z made up 25% of the U.S. population, making them a larger cohort than the Baby Boomers or Millennials. They will be the first to come of age after same-sex marriage was legalized nationally in the United States in 2015. And the first to overwhelmingly approve of same-sex marriage in their adolescence. They exhibit positive feelings about the increasing ethnic diversity in the U.S. and are more likely than older generations to have social circles that include people from different ethnic groups, races, and religions.

They are predominantly the children of Generation X, but they also may have parents who are Millennials. In much of the literature available, Generation Z is the least likely to believe that there is such a thing as the American Dream because their Generation X parentage, among adult generations, has demonstrated the least belief in the concept of the American Dream.

Digging deeper into this paradigm, the Great Recession of 2008 and after seeing their parents and older siblings struggle in the workforce, has taught them to be independent, and instilled a strong desire to remain so. What does this produce? A more conservative, more money-oriented, more entrepreneurial and pragmatic, personal belief system compared to Millennials.

Generation Z was the first generation to have widespread access to the Internet from early school age. With the web revolution that occurred throughout the 1990s, they have been exposed to an unprecedented amount of technology in their upbringing. As technology became more compact and affordable, the popularity of smartphones in the United States grew exponentially. With 77% of 12–17-year-olds owning a cell phone in 2015, technology has strongly influenced Generation Z in terms of communication and education. About three-quarters of 13–17-year-olds use their cell phones daily, more than they watch TV. It has become a primary tool for identity creation, to define who they are socially and interpersonally.

The use of social media has become integrated into the daily lives of most Generation Z, who have access to mobile technology. They use it regularly to keep in contact with friends and family, particularly those they see every day. It also helps them to strengthen bonds and to develop new ones as they interact with people who they otherwise would not have met in the real world. As a result, they spend more time on their smartphones and using social media, which has caused online relationship development to become a new generational norm.

Some more specifics on this fast-growing demographic:

Gen Z has inherited from their Gen X parents a sense of insecurity, independence, and skepticism. Gen Z is also the first generation to be raised in the era of smartphones and social media, meaning many don't remember a more unconnected world in which one couldn't be in conversation with anyone anywhere at any time. Meanwhile, for many members of this demographic, same-sex marriage is less of a controversial political issue than an entrenched legal right. And they're more likely than any preceding generation to have social circles that include people from different ethnic groups, races, and religions.

Gen Z sees themselves as entrepreneurial. Gen Z has a desire for independence that, in general, also appears much stronger than Millennials. Many are interested in starting their own company—an interest driven in part by the growing omnipresence of start-ups like Facebook and Uber. Given their lack of on-the-job experience, however, this may represent more idealism than realism. And—in an interesting paradox with to be determined long-term ramifications—growing up socializing on social media has taken away from them some of the face-to-face skills needed for entrepreneurialism.

For some, money takes a back seat also to their desire for learning and development, with 36 percent rating growth opportunities as more important than remuneration. But many forego or consider skipping post-secondary education immediately after high school and work instead because they fear taking on education-related debt.

A desire to job hop also emerged as a differentiator from other generations. Many current polls point to a belief that they should stay in their first job for three years or less as the appropriate amount of time to spend at their first employer. A friendly work environment and flexible hours are also priorities for Gen Z, who are eager to work and value opportunity. This means they're unusually interested in employer-sponsored development opportunities, often as a substitute for post-secondary training. Gen Z also expects employers to have not only a strong social media presence but also to offer opportunities to collaborate with colleagues online – robust digital platforms offering business at the speed of thought.

As such, employers will have to show how they can help Gen Z reach their most important career goals. By providing effective and frequent training, as well as professional development opportunities, employers can help them find a niche within the company and maintain a high level of engagement and retention.

Smart and prescient organization leaders are taking deliberate steps to break traditional notions of hierarchical structures to create opportunities for open communication—of particular appeal to Gen Z. They are increasingly taking a hard look at their corporate culture, and how it resonates with the employees, they hope to attract. From start-ups to established multinationals, the clients we work with are putting a greater focus on inclusiveness and transparency, as well as ways to encourage creative, innovative thinking across generations.

CHAPTER 6

BRINGING IT ALL TOGETHER

It's here that organizations can see the all-important vision of the future. A future where an engaged, multigenerational workplace is the vehicle by which organizations arrive at an internal culture that supports getting business results.

KEY CHARACTERISTICS OF A BUSINESS-DRIVEN MULTIGENERATIONAL WORKPLACE

- Leadership believes that the 5Rs of Talent Management (Right person, in the Right role, with the Right skills, at the Right time, at the Right cost) is a vital competitive advantage
- Talent is viewed as an organizational, not a departmental, asset
- Knowledge sharing and exchange of talent are strongly encouraged
- Continuous improvement and learning are esteemed company values
- Managers recognize that they must be actively involved in developing and coaching their employees
- The organization is flexible in meeting the needs of employees and deploying them effectively
- Employees take active ownership in their own development and career
- Great attention is placed on workplace environmental issues such as challenging work, developmental opportunities, improving engagement, and expanding collegial relationships
- A dedication to being a high-performance organization, keeping standards high and only hiring exceptional employees

Now, the question is how to start driving these values throughout the organization and have them become ingrained into the culture. This isn't a quick process. Cultural change takes several years to accomplish in the best of situations, but it certainly won't happen unless intentional efforts are made over a concerted period.

Organizations that effectively engage the four generations of their employees realize a significant advantage over competitors — including performance gains that lead directly to improved financial results.

Without a strategic approach to bridging the generational gaps, including the different aspects of focus on employee engagement, many companies fail to ensure employees are satisfied in their roles and committed to achieving key strategic goals — risking turnover of key players in the Generation X and Millennial generations, and the inability to meet overall business objectives.

Adding to this challenge is the fact that many disengaged workers are actively seeking new opportunities as the economy grows, while competitors are looking for ways to gain an edge by pursuing restless Gen X and Millennial high performers.

Growth remains a top strategic priority for nearly half of all organizations, while many continue to focus on profitability. Innovation, efficiency and high-quality performance will be key to success. It's these traits that are present in the younger two generations, but a lack of engagement and loss of talent will seriously impact organizations in their ability to meet strategic objectives.

Organizations cannot afford to neglect employee engagement or not mind generation gaps. The costs to the organization can be significant. Losing key players means spending money to recruit, train, and get new employees. It could also mean declines in productivity, lost business opportunities and weakened customer relationships. Employee turnover impacts other employees as well, contributing to increased workloads and stress, further eroding engagement and creating an environment of discontent.

Organizations often seek a silver bullet. But the reality is that engaging and retaining talent requires a strategic, focused approach that demands an investment of time and resources. Executed well and driven by leadership, engaging your multigenerational employees is essential to achieving business performance and competitive advantage.

To mind the gap, it requires regularly assessing engagement levels within the organization. Understand key drivers unique to your workers. Gather as much information as possible on current engagement and retention initiatives and identify program strengths and weaknesses. Make incremental changes. Don't throw out what's yielding results, and modify programs that aren't working. Reward performance with innovative development programs—that really differentiate your high performers—they earned it and deserve it.

If your organization has had to cut costs and reduce investments in talent development programs, be sure employees understand the business rationale and what other initiatives will be available to support their career goals. Help employees to see how their roles and contributions to the organization fit together with the company's overall business goals.

In today's challenging economy, companies need to continue to manage costs while pursuing new market opportunities. With hiring expected to remain weak, growth must be driven by an organization's current employees. Minding the generation gap is now imperative for every organization. Organizations need now more than ever to invest in developing employee skills and competencies today—increasing productivity and performance that will drive sustainable growth tomorrow.

MOTIVATION, VALUES, AND RECOGNITION

Most employees (of all generations) do not get enough positive recognition at work. Cultivating an environment that supports it is one of the most impactful things any leader can do. This idea may sound deceptively simple but also represent a good start in helping employees to manage their stress so that they can come to work and contribute on at their highest level. But by no means is this a comprehensive list. For reducing stress through small, everyday efforts, the possibilities are endless. The most critical piece is to make it a consistent, focused part of an overall business strategy understanding that your bottom-line results rely on doing it well.

Organizations face adopting changes that address the shift from a Baby Boomer focused environment to a Millennial environment. Managers and leaders must consider evolving policies to keep pace with changing organizational cultures influenced by the Millennials as the largest generational cohort in the workplace. Keeping pace with the Baby Boomer and Millennial demographic change is an important consideration given the potentially harmful aspect of change from knowledge or skills deficits associated with organizational success.

On average, Millennials have overtaken Baby Boomers as the largest generational cohort in the workplace. Managers in all organizations will be tasked with managing this transition of generational dominance. Plenty of research exists discussing the different generations in the workplace and how changes to the workplace can accommodate Millennials. The increasing number of retiring Baby Boomers (actual and expected) within the next five years has created a gap in assessing the impact of their departure on organizational culture. The change from a Baby Boomer-centric workplace to a Millennial centric workplace will influence the corporate culture.

The influx of Generation Z, coupled with the shrinking presence of Baby Boomers is the impetus to organizational culture evolution. In terms of numbers alone, the shift of dominance from Baby Boomers to Millennials is forcing organizations to look at existing policies and processes to meet employees' needs. One term used to describe this organizational culture evolution is "millennializing" the workplace. Millennializing calls for managers and leaders to consider evolving policies that cater more to Millennials as the largest generational cohort in the workplace.

The importance of understanding values and characteristics of the different generations, and how organizational culture is impacted, is paramount to navigating organizational culture change. The literature is unclear on whether the values of Millennials are more closely aligned to Generation Xers or to Baby Boomers. Nevertheless, baby boomers and millennials have common values that warrant consideration. There is a pending awareness between baby boomers and millennials of each other's multigenerational differences is a positive step in coping with generational apertures.

Generational differences can be the primary drivers of organizational change. Although the Millennials and Generation Z are unique in their individual ways, each generational cohort is capable of being influenced or doing the influencing. Millennials are likely to be affected by Generation Xers, just as Generation Xers were likely to be influenced by Baby Boomers when they first entered the workforce.

A common theme that emerged in my research is that the different values exhibited by Millennials are often a source of conflict, hurting existing group dynamics dominated by a Baby Boomer-centric environment. A positive perspective on the differences presented by Millennials in the workplace: new aspects are often the source of innovation that fuels organizational culture changes; capitalizing on generational differences is accomplished by stratagems that embrace generational differences and acceptance.

Multigenerational interaction influences organizational and generational culture, and the intermingling of different value systems can lead to conflict. Multigenerational worker interaction requires an understanding of workplace expectations established by organizational values and goals. Baby boomers and millennials are expected to adapt and follow cultural and value norms. Thus, value differences between Millennials and Baby Boomers will influence workplace processes to facilitate member negotiation.

Leaders shape organizational culture with their goal set on generating positive change that promotes success, one that encompasses Baby Boomer and Millennial values. Identifying the right reward for each generation significantly influences the retention of star employees. The dichotomy of values and experiences provides a different lens to view the work environment. For example, one common Baby Boomer belief is that gaining a prominent position in the workplace is something that is earned and validated by visible efforts. The value system of Millennials, upon entering the organization and at the earlier stage of their career, includes the goal of making an impact and gaining recognition. Baby Boomers, most likely entering the last stages of their career, have already contributed to organizational success and failure.

Adding to this paradigm is how the modern business environment has become increasingly complex. There are four unique generational cohorts in the workplace. The rapidly changing business environment presents challenges involving multigenerational diversity. The different values, attitudes, and beliefs of these generational cohorts may affect productivity. Opportunities and challenges emerge as generational diversity increases in the multigenerational workforce. The focus of this study was to explore strategies managers could use to motivate a multigenerational workforce.

The modern workforce comprises four generations: Baby Boomers, Generation X, Millennials, and Gen Z. Each of these generational cohorts has different factors that motivate them. Generational cohort contributes to personality and working styles that create challenges for leadership. Employee motivation affects all aspects of business. Therefore, it is imperative that managers understand how to motivate a multigenerational workforce. This is catching many managers flat-footed with a lack of strategies to motivate a multigenerational workforce. The primary role of business leaders is to encourage employees and manage conflict. Lack of employee motivation can lead to increased absenteeism, decreased productivity, high turnover, and reduced profits. Motivating across generational boundaries is creating challenges for leadership.

Understanding what motivates the multigenerational workforce could foster increased acceptance and appreciation for the different generations in the workforce. Five generations of workers actively share the workforce for the first time in history, and each of these generational cohorts has various factors that motivate them.

Organizations and leaders have failed to address generational work-value differences. And this has resulted in low organizational morale, increased turnover, and reduced profits. Organizations will be less competitive globally if they do not capitalize on the strengths generational diversity can bring to the workplace, such as the sharing of perspectives leading to creativity and innovation. Managers formulate workforce planning practices and human-resource-management strategies based on their beliefs that work values are related to generational differences. It can be argued that managers need to examine why and how differences between the generations impact competencies, behaviors, attitudes, and other attributes to ensure their recruitment, management strategies, and practices.

The goal is to appropriately address the differences and do not lead to unintended consequences, such as creating or inviting greater generational conflict in the workplace.

CONCLUSION

GETTING TO KNOW YOUR MULTIGENERATIONAL WORKFORCE

Your workforce is changing rapidly. While Baby Boomers are staying in the job market longer, Gen Xer and Millennials are struggling to move up the corporate ladder. At the same time, Gen Z is coming into the workplace with different expectations while fresh out of college. All in all, we are moving into the Millennial majority workforce.

To engage this multigenerational workforce and retain the top talent, you need to adapt your talent management strategies now to respond to your peoples' changing needs.

By looking at what drives people engagement, you can clearly see differences in what each generation values and what they look for in an employer. While your Boomers sought good paying jobs, recognition, and status, your Millennials and Gen Z new hires want to be part of a diverse team, learn new things every day, have more flexibility to manage their lives and interact with people through social media. Identifying these differences and addressing them proactively will help you retain top talent.

Recruitment techniques need to move beyond the traditional interview into assessment centers, profiling and other methods to help get a fuller picture of the capabilities of the people you are hiring. If you're not connected daily to potential recruits through social media, then you're missing out on some of the top talent.

Your recruiters should be using social media sites as key sources for finding non-active job seekers. Not only will these potential recruits learn about your organization, but you'll also learn a lot about them from their social media profile. To assess talent, focus on the candidate profile your organization needs for the future, which is moving much more toward leadership capabilities and less on technical skills. Qualities like being able to adapt to change, understanding and supporting team roles and being flexible are increasingly important.

Millennials need to feel emotionally connected to their place of work to be engaged and to stay. They don't expect their employers to manage their career or provide them with job security but do expect learning and development opportunities, engaging work and flexibility in how they work. Leaders need to adapt to this style of working. Learning about what this generation needs from you, and monitoring how well you're doing is how you can demonstrate to your Millennials that you value them and want them to stay. Retention, for Millennials, is founded on four key drivers: a flexible work environment, engaging work and development opportunities, a sense of community and competitive pay. Are you supporting these drivers by ensuring your organization promotes flexibility, learning opportunities, and the ability to give back to the community and by offering competitive compensation? Excessive and prolonged work hours have been found to predict higher turnover, lower commitment, and reduced job satisfaction. It harms people's commitment to their job and may even influence their choice to leave, and this is even more pronounced with top performers and Millennials.

How are you addressing this imbalance? Different ways to manage your workforce through, for example, offering flexible work hours, flexible time off programs and supplementing your workforce during peak periods with contingent workers, are a few ways to address this issue to mitigate the risk of losing your top talent.

THE 5RS OF TALENT MANAGEMENT FOR LEADERS

The November 2012 address by Cynthia Trudell of PepsiCo to the Graziadio School of Business and Management at Pepperdine University is something I found striking and important. It resonated deeply with me for two reasons: First, because Pepperdine is my alma mater, having graduated from the Graduate School of Education Psychology with my doctorate in 2009. Second, because the philosophy of the 5Rs to talent management is one that I ascribe to in leading my Boston-based consultancy.

Ms. Trudell discusses that although HR at PepsiCo was doing many things well, and we were always there for their internal clients—they set their sights on helping their businesses achieve what she called the Five Rs: having the right people in the right place at the right time doing the right work the right way. I substitute the last "R" in PepsiCo's perspective of "Right Way" with "Right Cost." Everything in business comes down to cost and cost can be used to measure current and future success.

The 5Rs also have a strong connection to my last book, where I espouse twenty keys for leaders to use in mastering the top priority of leadership– connecting with people.

It has always been the people. Without them, what's a leader? What's an organization? It's a fact that leaders in the 21st century are faced with many challenges that previous generations never had: expanding global competition, a surge in loss of intellectual resources with the wave of coming Boomer retirements, and a workforce with different generational values. To lead effectively, you have to understand those you lead. And to best do that, I offer five keys to effective leadership that connect to the 5Rs of talent management:

1) Right People: Coach and Mentor to Cultural Fit, Not to Job Function

Developing and sustaining a positive and productive culture requires that people "fit." It's not just about talent or experience alone; you must make sure that the person you hire can align with the culture.

2) Right Roles: Be Agile, Not Fragile

You have to be flexible and willing to learn to be an effective leader. If you can't make the right decisions because you're unwilling to learn and adapt—then your leadership will fracture. You can't build a growing organization on a cracked foundation.

3) Right Skills: Make Professional Development a Contact Sport

Education is good, training is good, but real world experience is better. When developing yourself and/or your organization—look to the benefits that come from getting your hands dirty in the trenches. You'll come away with a stronger leader and will build a more effective and productive workforce with that understanding.

4) Right Time: Conduct Stay Interviews Often

Understand why people want to stay with your company rather than fixate on why some choose to go. This ties back to the impact the leader and/or organization make at the granular employee level. Odds are if it's unfavorable, then at some point, that person is going to leave, and not many (if any) of their answers will be of importance. Leaders and organizations are better served if they try to find out what makes people enjoy working for them or for the company. It's a reinforcement of the positives that eliminates the need for retroactive fixes of someone's perceived negatives regarding a leader or company and in the long run, proves to be far more important.

5) Right Cost: Accept Change as Frequent Visitor

Change is constant. In dealing with change, you can make mistakes, and these are often caused by internal politics, generational differences, and miscommunication. That last item also holds the key to minimizing and mitigating missteps—leaders must communicate clearly when it comes to expectations and execution of policies within the organization.

Make these action items the center of your preparation and mastery as a leader. Seek to influence and inspire, not to drive and direct. If you do, you'll connect with your people in a way to unlock your own door to be a more effective leader.

***

Just as talent needs are shifting, so too is the way business is conducted. Flexibility is important to all generations but is critical for Millennials. We see the rise of more and more virtual—not collocated—teams. This presents unique challenges for management regarding leading, coaching and general oversight of a team that they don't see, and who don't see each other in the workplace every day. What technology do you have in place to make work more efficient, productive and flexible and do your leaders trust their staff to be productive in a virtual workplace?

Having leaders who are comfortable working within, and are supportive of, a flexible culture is critical. This is a challenge for leaders who didn't grow up in that type of environment. Equally, the need to give continual recognition and appreciation for a job well done is crucial to the Millennial generation. Think of it as instantaneous feedback. For many leaders who were occasionally told they were doing a good job, this is another significant change to realize that Millennials need ongoing feedback and appreciation for their efforts.

Remember, for Millennials, and Gen Z, flexibility, and recognition are major drivers of commitment. So your corporate culture will need to adapt to reflect this trend.

Millennials and Gen Z employees will expect skill development in return for delivering high-quality work. They want to be continually learning and improving their skill sets. We continue to see a trend toward the gamification of learning solutions to adapt to this generation's needs.

It's a different approach to learning, and one many organizations are adopting.

To engage your workforce, what solutions do you have in place for developing your people on an ongoing basis? Take into consideration all of your options: formal and informal mentoring and other experiential learning opportunities, like job shadowing to help meet this growing need from your teams.

How people perceive their pay plays a key role in retention and job satisfaction. Millennials aren't as concerned with pay (providing the pay is competitive) and choose to stay with an organization for diverse reasons. Giving your Millennials more control over their career path, development opportunities and work/life flexibility are things to keep in mind to retain them.

In a relatively healthy job market, top performing Millennials can and may go elsewhere—either for an environment that they perceive will help them grow professionally or improved work/life flexibility. Due to improvements in technology and increased ease of mobility, competition for the top talent continues to be a challenge.

If you don't stay vigilant and continue to find ways to adapt to and support your changing workforce needs, you risk losing your best and brightest.

Become the type of leader that places more importance on employee individual performance and less on their title. Most importantly—treat yourself the same way. Don't get puffed up because of your title or position. Instead, show everyone that you deserve respect by who you are, how inclusive you can be to the generations in your workforce. And what you do to make your employees feel welcomed and valued, as they contribute to the organization in a place that allows them to be their authentic self.

Do these things well as a leader... and you will indeed mind the gap by getting business results in a multigenerational workforce.

WORKS CONSULTED

Al-Asfour, A., & Lettau, L. (2014). Strategies for leadership styles for the multigenerational workforce. Journal of Leadership, Accountability and Ethics, 11, 58-70. Retrieved from www.na-businesspress.com

Anantatmula, V. S., & Shrivastav, B. (2012). Evolution of project teams for generation y workforce. International Journal of Managing Projects In Business, 5(1), 9-26.

Andert, D. (2011). Alternating leadership as a proactive organizational intervention: Addressing the needs of Baby Boomers, Generation Xers, and Millennials. Journal of Leadership, Accountability and Ethics, 8, 67-83. Retrieved from www.na- businesspress.com

Andrea, B., Gabriella, H., & Tímea, J. (2016). Y and Z generations at workplaces. Journal of Competitiveness, 8, 90-106.

Arsenault, P. (2004). Validating generational differences: A legitimate diversity and leadership issue. Leadership and Organization Development Journal, 12(2), 124-141.

Ashraf, N. (2012). Collaborating across generations. Strategic Communication Management, 16(2), 40-43. Retrieved from www.melcrum.com/SCM

Balda, J., & Mora, F. (2011). Adapting leadership theory and practice for the networked, Millennial generation. Journal of Leadership Studies, 5(3), 13-24.

Benson, J., & Brown, M. (2011). Generations at work: Are there differences and do they matter? International Journal of Human Resource Management, 22(9), 1843-1865.

Borrero, S., McGinnis, K., McNeil, M., Frank, J., & Conigliaro, R. (2008). Professionalism in residency training: Is there a generation gap? Teaching & Learning in Medicine, 20(1), 11-17.

Brody, C., & Rubin, B. (2011). Generational differences in the effects of insecurity, restructured workplace temporalities, and technology on organizational loyalty. Sociological Spectrum, 31(2), 163-192.

Brown, M. (2012). Responses to work intensification: does generation matter? International Journal of Human Resource Management, 23(17), 3578-3595.

Busch, P., Venkitachalam, K., & Richards, D. (2008). Generational differences in soft knowledge situations: Status, need for recognition, workplace commitment, and idealism. Knowledge and Process Management, 15(1) 45-58.

Carver, L., & Candela, L. (2008). Attaining organizational commitment across different generations of nurses. Journal of Nursing Management, 16(8), 984-991.

Clark, K. R. (2017). Managing multiple generations in the workplace. Radiologic Technology, 88, 379-398. Retrieved from https://www.ncbi.nlm.nih.gov

Cogin, J. (2012) Are generational differences in work values fact or fiction? Multi-country evidence and implications. The International Journal of Human Resource Management, 23(11), 2268-2294.

Connell, J. A., McMinn, N. E., & Bell, N. (2012). How will the next generation change the business world? A report on a survey. Insights To A Changing World Journal, 4, 100-113.

Costanza, D., Badger, J., Fraser, R., Severt, J., & Gade, P. (2012). Generational differences in work-related attitudes: A meta-analysis. Journal of Business & Psychology, 27(4), 375-394.

Coulter, J. S., & Faulkner, D. C. (2014). The multigenerational workforce. Professional Case Management, 19, 46-52.

Crumpacker, M., & Crumpacker, J. M. (2007). Succession planning and generational stereotypes: Should HR consider age-based values and attitudes a relevant factor or a passing fad? Public Personnel Management, 36(4), 349-369.

D'Amato, A., & Herzfeldt, R. (2008). Learning orientation, organizational commitment and talent retention across generations: A study of European managers. Journal of Managerial Psychology, 23(8), 929-953.

Day, A. (2007). Trading places: Problematizing the reverse ranking discourse of older worker-younger boss relationships. Florida Communication Journal, 36(2), 77-89.

Deal, J., Altman, D., & Rogelberg, S. (2010). Millennials at work: What we know and what we need to do (if anything). Journal of Business & Psychology, 25(2), 191-199.

Deal, J. J., Stawiski, S., Graves, L., Gentry, W. A., Weber, T. J., & Ruderman, M. (2013). Motivation at work: Which matters more, generation or managerial level? Consulting Psychology Journal: Practice & Research, 65(1), 1-16.

Deyoe, R. H., & Fox, T. L. (2011). Identifying strategies to minimize workplace conflict due to generational differences. Journal of Behavioral Studies In Business, 41-17. Retrieved from www.aabri.com/jbs

Eastland, R., Clark, K. (2015). Managing generational differences in radiology. Radiological Management, 37(3) 52-56. Retrieved from http://www.radiologymanagement-digital.com

Ehrhart, K., Mayer, D. M., & Ziegert, J. C. (2012). Web-based recruitment in the Millennial generation: Work–life balance, website usability, and organizational attraction. European Journal of Work & Organizational Psychology, 21(6), 850-874.

Eliasa, S. M., Smith, W. L., & Barneya, C. E. (2012). Age as a moderator of attitude towards technology in the workplace: work motivation and overall job satisfaction. Behaviour & Information Technology, 31(5), 453-467.

Erlam, G., Smythe, L., & Wright, V. (2016). Simulation and Millennials-The Perfect Storm. Open Journal of Nursing, 6, 688-698.

Ferri-Reed, J. (2010). The keys to engaging Millennials. Journal for Quality and Participation, 33(1), 31-33.

Ferri-Reed, J. (2014). Millennializing the workplace. Journal for Quality and Participation, 36(1), 13-14. Retrieved from www.asq.org

Garnero, A., Kampelmann, S., & Rycx, F. (2014). The heterogeneous effects of workforce diversity on productivity, wages, and profits. Industrial Relations, 53, 430-477.

Gay, D. A., Lynxwiler, J. P., & Smith, P. (2015). Religiosity, spirituality, and attitudes towards same-sex marriage: A cross-sectional cohort comparison. Sage Open, 5(3), 1-14.

Gentry, W., Deal, J., Griggs, T., Mondore, S., & Cox, B. (2011). A comparison of generational differences in endorsement of leadership practices with actual leadership skill level. Consulting Psychology Journal: Practice & Research, 63(1), 39-49.

Glass, A. (2007). Understanding generational differences for competitive success. Industrial and Commercial Training, 39(2), 98-103.

Griffin, K. (2008). Metaphor, language, and organizational transformation. Organization Development Journal, 26(1), 89-97.

Griffin, L. (2004). "Generations and collective memory" revisited: Race, region, and memory of org/10.1177/000312240406900404 civil rights. American Sociological Review, 69(4), 544-557.

Gursoy, D., Geng-Qing Chi, C., & Kardag, E. (2013). Generational differences in work values and attitudes among frontline and service contact employees. International Journal of Hospitality Management, 32(13), 40-48.

Güss, C., Burger, M., & Dörner, D. (2017). The role of motivation in complex problem-solving. Frontiers in Psychology, 8, 851.

Hanks, R., & Icenogle, M. (2001). Preparing for an age-diverse workforce: Intergenerational service learning in social gerontology and business curricula. Educational Gerontology, 27(1), 49-70.

Hartman, J. L., & McCambridge, J. (2011). Optimizing Millennials' communication styles. Business Communication Quarterly, 74(1), 22-44.

Haeger, D. L., & Lingham, T. (2014). A trend toward work-life fusion: A multigenerational shift in technology use at work. Technology Forecasting and Social Change, 89(1), 1-10.

Hernaus, T., & Mikulic, J. (2014). Work characteristics and work performance of knowledge workers. Euromed Journal of Business, 9, 268-292.

Hershatter, A., & Epstein, M. (2010). Millennials and the world of work: An organization and management perspective. Journal of Business and Psychology, 25(2), 211-223.

Higginson, N. (2010). Preparing the next generation for the family business: Relational factors and knowledge transfer in mother-to-daughter succession. Journal of Management and Marketing Research, 41-18.

Hillman, D. R. (2014). Understanding multigenerational work-value conflict resolution.

Journal of Workplace Behavioral Health, 29, 24-257.

Holian, R. (2015). Work, career, age, and life-stage: Assumptions and preferences of a multigenerational workforce. Labour and Industry, 25, 278-292. [SEP]

Hobman, E. and Bordia, P. (2006). The role of team identification in the dissimilarity—conflict relationship. Group Processes and Intergroup Relations, 9(4), 483-507.

Hokanson, C., Sosa-Fey, J., & Vinaja, R. (2011). Mitigating the loss of knowledge resulting from the attrition of younger generation employees. International Journal of Business & Public Administration, 8(2), 138-151.

Ismail, M., & Lu, H. S. (2014). Cultural values and career goals of the Millennial generation: An integrated conceptual framework. Journal of International Management Studies, 9, 38-50.

Jehn, K., Chadwick, C., & Thatcher, S. (1997). To agree or not to agree: The effects of value congruence, individual demographic dissimilarity, and conflict on workgroup outcomes. International Journal of Conflict Management, 8(4), 287-305.

Jobe, L. L. (2014). Generational differences in work ethic among three generations of registered nurses. Journal of Nursing Administration, 44, 303-308.

Johnson, M., Johnson, L. (2016). Signposts: Harbingers of things to come. Generations, incorporated: From Boomers to Linksters – Managing the friction between generations at work. New York, NY: AMACOM.

Johnson, J., & Lopes, J. (2008). The intergenerational workforce revisited. Organization Development Journal, 26(1), 31-36.

Jones, S. (2017). Succession planning: Creating a case for hiring new graduates. Nursing Economic$, 35(2), 64-87. Retrieved from https://insights.ovid.com

Joshi, A., Dencker, J. C., & Franz, G. (2011). Generations in organizations. Research In Organizational Behavior, 31177-205.

Kaifi, B. A., Nafei, W. A., Khanfar, N. M., & Kaifi, M. M. (2012). A multigenerational workforce: Managing and understanding Millennials. International Journal of Business & Management, 7(24), 88-93.

Kilber, J., Barclay, A., & Ohmer, D. (2014). Seven tips for managing Generation Y. Journal of Management Policy and Practice, 15, 80-91.

Kiyonaga, N. B. (2004). Today is the tomorrow you worried about yesterday: Meeting the challenges of a changing workforce. Public Personnel Management, 33(4), 357.

Kowske, B., Rasch, R., & Wiley, J. (2010). Millennials' (lack of) attitude problem: An empirical examination of generational effects on work attitudes. Journal of Business and Psychology, 25(2), 265-279.

Krahn, H. J., & Galambos, N. L. (2014) Work values and beliefs of 'Generation X' and 'Generation Y.' Journal of Youth Studies 17, 92-112.

Kultalahti, S., & Viitala, R. L. (2014). Sufficient challenges and a weekend ahead- Generation Y describing work. Journal of Organizational Change Management. 27, 569-582.

Lather, P., & St. Pierre, E. A. (2013). Post-qualitative research. International Journal of Qualitative Studies in Education, 26, 629-633.

Lawson, M. (2017). Shifting to a next generation workplace: Aurora, Colorado, creates a model for attracting and retaining young talent. Public Management, 1, 14. Retrieved from https://icma.org

Lester, S. W., Standifer, R. L., Schultz, N. J., & Windsor, J. M. (2012). Actual versus perceived generational differences: An empirical examination. Journal of Leadership & Organizational Studies, 19, 341-354.

Lester, S. W., Standifer, R. L., Schultz, N. J., & Windsor, J. M. (2012). Actual versus perceived generational differences at work: An empirical examination. Journal of Leadership & Organizational Studies, 19(3), 341-354.

Levenson, A. (2010). Millennials and the world of work: An economist's perspective. Journal of Business and Psychology, 25(2), 257-264.

Locke, L., Silverman, S., & Spirduso, W. (2010). Reading and understanding research (3rd ed.).Thousand Oaks, CA: Sage.

Loveland, E. (2017). Instant generation. The Journal of College Admission, 34-38.

Lyons, S., & Kuron, L. (2014). Generational differences in the workplace: A review of the evidence and directions for future research. Journal of Organizational Behavior, 35, 139-157.

Lyons, S., Higgins, C., & Duxbury, L. (2007). An empirical assessment of generational differences in basic human values. Psychological Reports, 101(2), 339-352.

Lyons, S. T., Schweitzer, L., Ng, E. W., & Kuron, L. J. (2012). Comparing apples to apples: A qualitative investigation of career mobility patterns across four generations. Career Development International, 17(4), 333-357.

Macky, K., Gardner, D., & Forsyth, S. (2008). Generational differences at work: Introduction and overview. Journal of Managerial Psychology, 23(8), 857-861.

Maier, T. A. (2011). Hospitality leadership implications: Multigenerational perceptions of dissatisfaction and intent to leave. Journal of Human Resources In Hospitality & Tourism, 10(4), 354-371.

Mannheim, Karl. 1929. Ideology and Utopia. London: Routledge.

Masibigiri, V., & Nienaber, H. (2011). Factors affecting the retention of Generation X public servants: An exploratory study. South African Journal of Human Resource Management, 9(1), 44-54.

McDonald, P. (2008). The multigenerational workforce. Internal Auditor, 65(5), 60-67. Retrieved from www.theiia.org/intauditor

Maslow, A. (1943). A theory of human motivation. Classics in organization theory (6th ed.). Belmont, CA: Wadsworth Press.

Mencl, J., & Lester, S. W. (2014). More alike than different: What generations value and how the values affect employee workplace perceptions. Journal of Leadership & Organizational Studies, 21, 257-272.

Mikkelsen, M. F., Jacobsen, C. B., & Andersen, L. B. (2017). Managing employee motivation: Exploring the connections between managers' enforcement actions, employee perceptions, and employee intrinsic motivation. International Public Management Journal, 20, 183-205.

Murphy, W. (2012) Reverse mentoring at work: Fostering cross-generational learning and developing Millennial leaders. Human Resource Management, 51(4), 549- 573.

Neyer, L., & Yelinek, K. (2011). Beyond Boomer meets Nextgen: Examining mentoring practices among Pennsylvania academic librarians. Journal of Academic Librarianship, 37(3), 215-221.

Outten, M. K. (2012). From veterans to nexters: Managing a multigenerational nursing workforce. Nursing Management, 43(4), 42-47.

Parry, E., & Urwin, P. (2011). Generational differences in work values: A review of theory and evidence. International Journal of Management Reviews, 13, 79-96.

Rawlins, C., Indvik, J., & Johnson, P. (2008). Understanding the new generation: What the Millennial cohort absolutely, positively must have at work. Journal of Organizational Culture, Communications, and Conflict, 12(2), 1-8.

Redmond, Paul (2017). Talking about my generation: Exploring the benefits engagement challenge. Retrieved from https://wealth.barclays.com

Reisenwitz, T., & Iyer, R. (2009). Differences in Generation X and Generation Y: Implications for the organization and marketers. Marketing Management Journal, 19(2), 91-103.

Sessa, V. I., Kabacoff, R. I., Deal, J., & Brown, H. (2007). Generational differences in leader values and leadership behaviors. The Psychologist-Manager Journal, 10(1), 47-74.

Sias, P. M., Pedersen, H., Gallagher, E. B., & Kopaneva, I. (2012). Workplace friendship in the electronically connected organization. Human Communication Research, 38(3), 253-279.

Simons, N. (2010). Leveraging generational work styles to meet business objectives. Information Management Journal, 44(1), 28-33.

Sirias, D., Karp, H., & Brotherton, T. (2007). Comparing the levels of individualism/ collectivism between Baby Boomers and Generation X: Implications for teamwork. Management Research News, 30(10), 749-761.

Smith, T. J. (2015). Understanding the Millennial generation. Journal of Financial Service Professionals, 69(6), 11-14.

Smola, K., & Sutton, C. (2002). Generational differences: Revisiting generational work values for the new millennium. Journal of Organizational Behavior, 23(4), 363.

Solaja, O., & Ogunola, A. (2016). Leadership style and multigenerational workforce: A call for workplace agility in Nigerian public organizations. International Journal of African and Asian Studies, 21, 46-56.

Sonnentag, S., Unger, D., & Nagel, I. J. (2013). Workplace conflict and employee wellbeing: The moderating role of detachment from work during off-job time. International Journal of Conflict Management, 24, 166-183.

Stanton, R. (2017). Communicating with employees: Resisting the stereotypes of generational cohorts in the workplace. IEEE Transactions on Professional Communication, 3, 256.

Stephens, K. K., Cho, J. K., & Ballard, D. I. (2012). Simultaneity, sequentiality, and speed: Organizational messages about multiple-task completion. Human Communication Research, 38(1), 23-47.

Strange, C. (2004). Constructions of student development across the generations. New Directions For Student Services, 106, 47-57.

Tembo, A. C., Parker, V., & Higgins, I. (2013). The experience of sleep deprivation in intensive care patients: Findings from a larger hermeneutic phenomenological study. Intensive and Critical Care Nursing, 29, 310-316.

Torronen, J. (2014). Situational, cultural and societal identities: Analyzing subject positions as classifications, participant roles, viewpoints, and interactive positions. Journal for the Theory of Social Behavior, 44, 80-98.

Turner, A. (2015). Generation Z: Technology and social interest. Journal of Individual Psychology, 71, 103-113.

Twenge, J., & Campbell, S. (2008). Generational differences in psychological traits and their impact on the workplace. Journal of Managerial Psychology, 23(8), 862- 877.

Twenge, J. M., Campbell, W. K., & Freeman, E. C. (2012). Personality processes and individual differences: Generational differences in young adults' life goals, concern for others, and civic orientation, 1966-2009. Journal of Personality and Social Psychology, 102, 1045-1062.

Twenge, J., Campbell, S., Hoffman, B., & Lance, C. (2010). Generational differences in work values: Leisure and extrinsic values increasing, social and intrinsic values decreasing. Journal of Management, 36(5), 1117-1142.

Twenge, J. (2010). A review of the empirical evidence on generational differences in work attitudes. Journal of Business and Psychology, 25(2), 201-210.

Wilson, B., Squires, M., Widger, K., Cranley, L., & Tourangeau, A. (2008). Job satisfaction among a multigenerational nursing workforce. Journal of Nursing Management, 16(6), 716-723.

Wong, M., Gardiner, E., Lang, W., & Coulon, L. (2008). Generational differences in personality and motivation. Do they exist and what are the implications for the workplace? Journal of Managerial Psychology, 23(8), 878-890.

Zopiatis, A., Krambia-Kapardis, M., & Varnavas, A. (2012). Y-ers, X-ers, and Boomers: Investigating the multigenerational (mis)perceptions in the hospitality workplace. Tourism & Hospitality Research, 12(2), 101-121.

ABOUT THE AUTHOR

Dr. Curtis Odom is Managing Partner of Prescient Strategists, President of Stuck On Start Coaching, and Executive Professor of Management and Organizational Development at Northeastern University.

Prescient Strategists is an international award-winning management consulting practice to Fortune 100 companies, colleges, and universities. Our advisory services focus on delivering change management, organizational culture, executive coaching, and leadership development solutions to clients during mergers and acquisitions, and complex business transformation initiatives.

Stuck On Start Coaching provides clients with customized offerings that equip their leaders to effectively manage and lead today's multigenerational, diverse workforce. Stuck On Start Coaching partners with organizations to develop successful strategies to onboard recent college graduates, and solutions to best engage and retain top talent within their culture.

Dr. Odom is an Executive Professor of Management and Organizational Development at Northeastern University. His passion for teaching is on display in the classroom during his Organizational Behavior, or Management Consulting lectures students where he teaches his students how to "play the corporate culture game" and win. His ability to connect content to context is born of a career of over 20 years as a corporate executive, serial entrepreneur, consultant, practitioner, researcher, published author, and executive coach. His diverse career in industry is preceded by a 10-year active duty military career serving proudly in the United States Navy to also include being deployed during Operation Desert Storm.

As a testament to his professional brand, Curtis was honored internationally as the Post-Merger Integration Advisor of The Year (USA) for 2016 by Corporate LiveWire. Local to Boston, Curtis was also awarded the high distinction of being selected as a member of the Boston Business Journal's Top 40 Under 40 class for 2010.

Curtis is the author of four books, *Mind The Gap: Getting Business Results in Multigenerational Organizations, Generation X Approved: Top 20 Keys to Effective Leadership, Stuck in the Middle: A Generation X View of Talent Management*, and his new book, *From Campus to*

Corner Office: How Co-Ops and Internships Will Help You Win in the Workplace has debuted to rave reviews.

Website: www. StuckOnStartCoaching.com

Email: dco@stuckonstartcoaching.com

www.ingramcontent.com/pod-product-compliance
Lightning Source LLC
Chambersburg PA
CBHW032005190326
41520CB00007B/361